THE DILEMMAS OF DEVELOPMENT WORK
Ethical challenges in regeneration

Paul Hoggett, Marjorie Mayo and Chris Miller

This edition published in Great Britain in 2009 by

The Policy Press
University of Bristol
Fourth Floor
Beacon House
Queen's Road
Bristol BS8 1QU
UK

Tel +44 (0)117 331 4054
Fax +44 (0)117 331 4093
e-mail tpp-info@bristol.ac.uk
www.policypress.org.uk

North American office:
The Policy Press
c/o International Specialized Books Services (ISBS)
920 NE 58th Avenue, Suite 300
Portland, OR 97213-3786, USA
Tel +1 503 287 3093
Fax +1 503 280 8832
e-mail info@isbs.com

British Library Cataloguing in Publication Data
A catalogue record for this book is available from the British Library.

Library of Congress Cataloging-in-Publication Data
A catalog record for this book has been requested.

ISBN 978 1 86134 971 2 paperback
ISBN 978 1 86134 972 9 hardcover

Cover design by Qube Design Associates, Bristol.
Front cover: image kindly supplied by www.alamy.com
Printed and bound in Great Britain by Hobbs the Printers, Southampton.

For Jeremy Brent (1950–2006):

Youth worker, intellectual and trade unionist

Contents

Acknowledgements

Our thanks go to the community workers, youth workers and others who enthusiastically participated in the research on which a good deal of this book is based. In this regard we must also register our appreciation to the Economic and Social Research Council, who funded the research (ref no RES-000-23-0127), and to Phoebe Beedell and Luis Jimenez, who were employed as researchers during the data-gathering phases of the project. We are also grateful to those who served on the Advisory Board for this project and to Pam Smith and Sarah Banks, whose ideas proved very helpful after the project was over as we were writing the book. Finally our thanks to Julia Long and Glynis Morrish for all the secretarial support they provided.

Some parts of this book draw upon articles which have previously appeared elsewhere. Chapter Five draws on P. Hoggett, M. Mayo and C. Miller, 'Private passions, the public good and public service reform', (2006) *Social Policy and Administration*, vol 40, no 7, pp 758–73. Chapter Six draws on P. Hoggett, M. Mayo and C. Miller, 'Individualization and ethical agency' in Cosmo Howard (ed), *Contested Individualization: Debates About Contemporary Personhood* (Palgrave Macmillan, 2008). Chapter Seven draws on P. Hoggett, M. Mayo and C. Miller, 'Relations of authority', (2006) *Organisational & Social Dynamics*, vol 6, no 2, pp 224–40. Chapter Nine draws on M. Mayo, P. Hoggett and C. Miller, 'Navigating the contradictions of public service modernisation: the case of community engagement professionals', (2007) *Policy & Politics*, vol 35, no 4, pp 667–82.

ONE

Introduction

Changing nature of development work

Development work, broadly defined, has traditionally included a range of activities designed to strengthen the capacity of local groups and communities to identify and give effective voice to their needs, to draw in resources from public and private sources and to effect changes in the policies and strategies of government at local, regional and even national levels. Development work has focused on disadvantaged communities in both rural and urban areas and, as we demonstrate in more detail in Chapter Three, although its origins lay in work with the urban poor of industrialising nations at the beginning of the 20th century, it has since become a major intervention strategy in developing countries.

Typically in current usage, the term 'development' implies development in this latter sense, international development in the global South. In this book, however, we use the term more generically, exploring a range of policies and strategies to promote social change, with a particular focus on disadvantaged areas and communities, recognising that these are to be identified within as well as between national contexts, North and South. In parallel, throughout the book we refer to 'development professionals'. We use this in a similarly generic way to refer to all those workers, professionally qualified or not, who have social, community or neighbourhood development contained within their job descriptions or their remits as community representatives in structures of governance. In Britain – unlike the global South – there are very few workers who have the specific job title of 'development worker' (although there may be different patterns in other countries of the global North). The nearest to this job title in Britain would be that of 'community development worker', and community development workers feature in this book. But subsequent discussions are not confined to the roles, challenges and dilemmas of community development workers per se. In recent years, a growing number of professionals have been tasked with engaging with service users and with communities more broadly. From police officers to housing workers to healthcare professionals, teachers and planners, professionals are expected to spend various amounts of their time engaged in long-term development work, in this broad sense of the term. As writings on 'community practice' have demonstrated, the focus for community 'practitioners' has widened beyond professionals' remit to work with individual service users in relation to a specific need or problem, moving on to the task of strengthening the capacity of groups, organisations or neighbourhoods or facilitating the emergence of new groups or organisations, engaging with structures of governance (Banks et al, 2003).

While the terms 'community practice' and 'community professional' capture much of the essence of these changes, the focus on the 'professional' needs to be broadened for our purposes to include those whose involvement goes beyond their professional roles – for example, the teacher who has become a community representative because of his/her standing and involvement in community issues in the neighbourhood of their school. We also reflect on the appropriateness of the term 'community engagement', a term with increasing resonance in contemporary policy discourse in Britain. But this term has tended to be associated with government initiatives to promote community engagement, from the top down. We wanted to find a term that would also include community initiatives from the bottom up. So we decided to stay with our original formulation, concluding that 'development professional' best captures the essence of this work without allocating it to a specific job role. When we refer to 'development work' and 'development professionals', then, we use the term in this generic sense. When we refer to specific professions such as 'community development' or 'youth work', or when we refer to specific roles such as those of workers employed to promote regeneration, we use the relevant terms, reserving the terms 'development work' and 'development professionals' for broader, generic discussions.

Development work in disadvantaged communities has always posed significant ethical challenges for the development professionals involved. Given the location of such workers on the boundary between state and civil society these ethical challenges are partly inherent to the nature of the job. The work can at times involve a significant challenge to the state, as communities become involved in direct confrontations with government around issues ranging from slum clearance to action around the rights of women and children. But interestingly enough, in recent years, development work has become increasingly involved in the modernisation of governance itself. In Britain this has become foregrounded in strategic interventions to decentralise government, to engage citizens with the monitoring of agency performance and to connect citizens with service planning and service delivery as well as the traditional concern to address issues of poverty and social exclusion. For practitioners, these strategies involve increasing complexity and inherent tensions. They struggle to balance emergent audit cultures and the requirements of the new public management (NPM) (including requirements for quick, tangible and measurable outputs) with the need for flexibility and creativity, building community engagement through longer-term development strategies. These potential tensions are especially marked in socially and culturally heterogeneous communities in which different interests and value systems compete (Miller and Ahmad, 1997).

In this book we aim to reconnect our analysis of current developments with an important but dormant tradition in social policy research that has recognised the dilemmas inherent to policy implementation at 'street' or 'community' level in different contexts, including the US and Britain (Marris and Rein, 1972; Lipsky, 1980). This book updates this early theorisation of the dilemmas of implementation by drawing on reflections on contemporary professional ethics, rooted in debates in moral philosophy and political theory, current debates about the modernisation of governance and psycho-social perspectives on emotion, identity and ethical agency.

In moral philosophy there has also been a growing interest in how people act ethically in ambiguous and conflictual situations where there is 'no right thing to do' (Williams, 1973, 1981; Bauman, 1993). In such uncertain situations the individual often feels torn between the claims of different groups and decision taking and action can involve considerable anxiety, guilt and remorse. Applying this to the task of the development worker we argue that this kind of work is therefore both ethically and emotionally challenging and, to illuminate the latter, we draw on concepts from the sociology of the emotions (Hochschild, 1983) and the psychoanalytic perspectives of Melanie Klein and Wilfred Bion (Anderson, 1992).

We therefore seek to introduce some new ways of thinking about the challenges of development work, but all new developments draw on and are nourished by past traditions. The three authors of this book have been immersed in these traditions, and in particular the idea that community workers operate in that precarious location of being both 'in and against' the state (London Edinburgh Weekend Return Group, 1980). It follows that we share certain views and perspectives, for instance, about the nature of the state and structural inequalities while each of us also brings some uniquely different ways of thinking. In writing the book each of us took the lead on particular chapters, passing our first drafts on to our co-authors for their thoughts to which we then responded by producing further drafts, and so on, through a process of dialogue. So we do not pretend to write with a single voice in this book but rather different voices predominate at different points and at other times several voices might be present together.

Paul Hoggett worked in London's voluntary sector in the 1970s in a radical community mental health project called the Battersea Action and Counselling Centre. For many years he combined various forms of political and community activism with a passionate interest in psychoanalysis, for it seemed to him that very often injustice seemed to 'get inside' people, affecting their soul and sometimes breaking their spirit. Psychoanalysis seemed to be the only theory around which was willing to get to grips with the depth of human suffering. Moreover, he was struck by the ways in which many political and community groups engaged in behaviour which at times seemed quite irrational, practices which certainly undermined their potential effectiveness and which often seemed to contradict their espoused democratic and egalitarian values. This sparked his interest in groups and behaviour in groups. Working with groups was a way of keeping alive an engagement with practice that, as his direct political involvements declined, became increasingly important to him. Finally he decided to pursue training as a psychotherapist, which he completed a few years ago, thereby reconnecting to his original involvement in mental health. More recently all of these interests have converged around what, in Britain, is becoming known as psycho-social studies, a multidisciplinary approach to exploring the ways in which the social/political and the deep psychological interact. Paul currently directs the Centre for Psycho-Social Studies at the University of the West of England, Bristol.

Since starting work in the 1970s some aspects of the world, such as the extent of injustice and inequality, have remained starkly problematic or have become more polarised, while others, such as the increasing social diversity of a society like Britain, have changed remarkably. We have come to appreciate the sometimes complex interplay between class, culture, 'race' and gender. The collapse of communist states and the rise of postmodern theory has also led us to be more circumspect about universals such as the common good and, indeed, of community itself. We now recognise the diversity of different voices and experiences but this very diversity presents huge challenges for democratic practice. Who has the right to represent whom? Who speaks for whom? By whose criteria is a given practice a democratic one? There are no longer (m)any simple answers. Development workers are in the thick of this and it was this sense of them having to traverse this new, ambiguous, contested and shifting terrain which informed Paul's conceptual analysis in Chapter Two, and explorations of some of the dilemmas of practice in Chapters Five and Six.

Marjorie Mayo comes from a social policy and community development background. Drawing on Marxist and feminist analyses, she starts with a focus on the ways in which structural inequalities shape the opportunities and constraints for development work, arguing that a critical understanding of these is an essential prerequisite for effective practice. These perspectives have informed her approach to the analysis of the modernisation of governance and public services (Chapter Eight), together with the ways in which the modernisation agenda is being negotiated (Chapter Nine) and some possible implications (Chapter Ten).

While Marjorie came to the research that underpins the empirical evidence discussed in this book without a psychoanalytical background – with continuing reservations about aspects of psychoanalytical approaches – she values the importance of the concept of emotional labour, recognising the value of exploring the interconnections between the personal and the political, whether these connections are to be explored through the lens of second wave feminism, through Pierre Bourdieu's concept of the 'habitus', or both. Through the research process she has also been impressed by the ways in which the participants themselves explained their own motivations and values. With little if any prompting, they began by outlining their own formative experiences, exploring the influences of family and community as well as the subsequent influences of the workplace and political and community engagement. Without necessarily sharing some of the reflections that draw more explicitly on psychoanalytical perspectives, she values their contribution to the development of a more comprehensive and critical understanding of the dilemmas facing development workers, and the implications for how to develop progressive strategies forward, in the current context. Marjorie is currently Professor of Community Development at Goldsmiths College, University of London.

Chris Miller grew up on a post-1945 Bevan council estate in North East England. He failed every education test thrown his way until the age of 16 when he requested a transfer from a secondary modern 'sink' school to a grammar school where he did just enough to take up a degree in sociology and politics in 1968. As the son of a highly educated Polish army officer war refugee who found himself working in the dockyards and factories and a mother who escaped shop work to become an education welfare officer, he experienced first hand the internalisation of injustice and its corrosive destructive capacities. He trained as a social worker on a programme that on reflection attempted to provide a psycho-social understanding and was drawn simultaneously to both community development work and mental health while influenced by radical and Marxist politics. The relationship between structure and agency has continued to be an intellectual, professional and personal struggle ever since, reflecting on his early life experiences with his first encounter with sociological and political theoretical frameworks. He worked in local government as a community development worker and social worker and in the non-governmental sector for local organisations and an international development agency, as well as being actively involved in community politics. He has continued with his interest in things psycho-dynamic over the years as a social policy and development academic, teaching youth and community development workers and more recently public service managers, and has participated in Tavistock-based experiential events. He is a Professor of Social Work at Flinders University, Adelaide, Australia.

Working closely with people whether in groups, families or as individuals who have experienced significant and continuous disadvantage it is difficult not to despair at damaged or restricted lives and their capacity for further destruction while being full of admiration for the resilience and capacity of the many, often to their own detriment, to make something positive out of intolerable circumstances. Understanding the basis of such defended strategies and according recognition to the humanity of the other is the first step in a development process that offers the potential for progressive social and individual change within a sometimes overwhelmingly constraining socio-political and economic context. Yet community development itself as a largely state-sponsored activity is plagued by contradictory objectives and while espousing ambitious aspirations is limited in its practical possibilities. It is this experience and understanding of development that has helped shaped Chapter Three as well as the practice dilemmas highlighted in Chapters Four and Seven. To enable others to act, to make a difference requires a reflexive understanding of one's own motivation and capacity to act, and development workers must engage continuously with their own inner selves. Those who participated in our research very generously gave us some access to these personal and professional struggles and the values that shaped their practice, tolerating and even appreciating our reflections.

The research

The day-to-day challenges which make up the working lives of development workers are still relatively unresearched. Moreover, with a few exceptions (Banks, 1995, 1999, 2004) there are still few empirical studies of ethical agency in welfare and development work and little understanding of what helps and what constrains individuals in such situations. The research basis for this book comes from a 27-month Economic and Social Research Council (ESRC)-funded project entitled 'Negotiating ethical dilemmas in contested communities', which was completed in November 2005. The project involved extended contact with 30 development workers in two cities over a period of 18 months.

This research set out to explore the ways in which these development workers identified and addressed the challenges of their roles. Drawing on insights from psycho-social approaches to social research, the research aimed to develop our understanding of the ways in which development workers' own personal backgrounds and experiences – their unique biographies – interlinked with their motivations and values, as front-line development workers, engaging with the dilemmas of community practice, community development, youth work, regeneration work and community engagement as professionals active within structures of governance. The sample was selected, in each city, to include a range of front-line professionals engaged in development work, including professionals whose involvement had emerged from their main professional roles (such as roles involving community safety, or education, including community-based adult learning).

The development workers came from differing backgrounds and employment from the public, voluntary and community sector (selected to provide a range of contexts and experiences) and they included men and women from, as well as working with, black and minority ethnic (BME) communities as well as from white British communities. Beginning with a life history interview, each development worker was interviewed on up to six occasions so that their response to ethical challenges could be tracked as they occurred. This was followed by a series of group interviews and interviews with national actors and policy makers.

Despite the differences between the development workers who were involved, in terms of their backgrounds and experiences, a number of common factors emerged from the study, factors that struck the development workers themselves as key, when our initial findings were fed back to them. In particular, the significance of development workers' personal motivations, values and commitments was striking. So was the way in which these motivations, values and commitments impacted on their approaches as workers, together with the ways in which workers drew on their own personal strengths in coping with the dilemmas of their roles, in varying contexts. While the research findings re-enforced the relevance of a psycho-social approach, the findings also deepened our shared understandings, in turn. In subsequent chapters we draw on examples from this research to illustrate our arguments. But this was a two-way process – our arguments have also been developed more generally as a result of our engagement with this particular research. While the research for this project was carried out in Britain, the issues have far wider significance, we would suggest, with potential resonances for development work around the globe.

Structure of the book

Drawing on the ESRC research the book provides case studies and vignettes that vividly reveal the ethically complex and emotionally challenging nature of development work in multiply disadvantaged communities.

Chapter Two provides a broad conceptual foundation for what follows. It explores different (liberal, Marxist and other) perspectives on the nature of the relationship between state and civil society and introduces concepts and arguments from contemporary social theory (Zygmunt Bauman on modernity) and moral theory (Charles Taylor and Bernard Williams) that contribute to our understanding of ethical agency in ambiguous and contested contexts. We argue that governance in a socially diverse society exemplifies such ambiguous and contested territory. The framework offered by such contemporary theorists is compared with that provided by writers such as Antonio Gramsci and Paulo Freire, whose work provided guidance to earlier generations of development workers. We also reconnect with the earlier work of Michael Lipsky, and Peter Marris and Martin Rein and indicate how these writers were more in touch with the emotional dimension of the ethical challenges of this kind of work.

What used to be called 'community development' in Britain is now frequently termed 'social cohesion', 'regeneration work' or 'capacity building'. While development work is now commonly thought of as only applying to developing countries, in Britain and other OECD (Organisation for Economic Co-operation and Development) countries there are an increasing number of professional roles that now require a proficiency in development activities without these skills and capacities being formally recognised. In Chapter Three we argue for the continued value and relevance of the concept of 'development' and 'development worker' in Britain too. We briefly outline some of the key traditions and principles of development work both in Britain and overseas. We illustrate this through a detailed examination of some of the typical dilemmas that development workers face when doing the job.

Chapter Four draws on material from the life histories of development workers. What personal resources do they require to be able to cope with the ethical and emotional demands of the job? We explore concepts of resilience that highlight the internal (psychological) and external (social) resources that enable people to cope with stressful life events. We suggest that 'being a survivor' can itself become a crucial psychological resource. We argue that both professional and managerial support for development workers is often lacking, and this can compound the stresses of the job. We also explore some of the strategies that development workers deploy to cope with the demands of the job, in particular the need to manage the boundaries between self and role, and self and other. We also problematise prevailing positivistic models of evidence, effectiveness and success, arguing for a 'complex systems psychodynamic' approach that recognises the centrality of 'emotion work' and 'relation work' to the development task.

In Chapter Five we explore the types of values that development workers have and where these values come from. We argue that unlike some other public sector professions, so many development workers are motivated by more than an ethic of care. We examine the very strong sense of social justice that drives many of them and the mixture of compassion and anger underlying this. Their preoccupation with power, inequalities of power and the need for oppressed people to 'take the power' means that they are committed to a solidaristic rather than altruistic ethic. The implications of this for liberal notions of the public service ethic are examined.

The focus on values continues in Chapter Six, but here we focus on their role and function rather than on their content. In dilemmatic space there is no 'right thing to do' but one's values can provide a crucial resource for navigating a terrain that is ambiguous, shifting and contested. By using a detailed case study we examine the role of values in providing 'orientation' in moral space. We also examine the proposition that what is crucial is how these values are held – what we call 'moral narcissism' lies at the root of many abuses of professional power. The chapter introduces the idea of personal capacities, something different to skills and therefore requiring a different approach to learning and development.

Development workers are immersed in complex power *and* authority relations. These terms are often confused but an understanding of what is distinct about each is vital for development work. Chapter Seven looks at some of the dilemmas of authority and power that typically face development workers and gives examples of how they have attempted to handle these. We argue that authority can assume different forms – positional, reputational and personal. We focus in particular on the latter by introducing the concept of self-authorisation that, we argue, is a vital capacity in development work. Again, using examples from people's life histories, we examine the roots of this important personal capacity.

The second part of the book moves on to explore the specific implications of public service modernisation. Chapter Eight situates our analysis in the context of the changing relationship between state and civil society with a particular focus on Blair's Britain. Labour's 'modernisation agenda' is situated in terms of processes of public service reform that were first set in train under Margaret Thatcher. Two dimensions of modernisation under Labour are considered – as a set of policies designed to address the perceived social problems relating to young people and disadvantaged communities and as a strategy for institutional change. Development workers involved in regeneration are both agents of modernisation (spearheading community governance, for example) and objects of modernisation (subject to the same processes of managerialisation as other public sector professions, for example). We highlight the inconsistencies and contradictions of modernisation and the way in which this therefore contributes to the dilemmas that development workers face.

The modernisation agenda construes spatial and other communities as both a problem and a solution. As a problem they are the site for 'out of control' young people, cycles of deprivation and conflictual community relations. As a solution they are the vehicles for public sector reform and will step into the democratic deficit left by the emasculation of local government. Thus, ostensibly, they become the harbingers of community governance and the new 'localism' that has been advocated by all three major political parties in Britain. There are powerful parallels with decentralisation strategies pursued in development contexts in the South. But the voluntary and statutory organisations and the international and local non-governmental organisations (NGOs) that employ development workers are themselves the objects of modernisation. As a consequence, the profession is subject to the same contradictory pressures involving competition and bureaucratisation as others. Chapter Nine examines the ways in which workers are able to keep doing effective development work *despite* the contradictions of government policies. How do they respond to attempts to managerialise the job, collaborate with agencies that are also competitors, establish a 'bottom line' beyond which they will not go? The chapter concludes by considering whether the profession has reached a 'tipping point' beyond which development work simply becomes a form of project management in an environment where workers and agencies are fragmented and divided.

The concluding chapter makes the case for the continuing importance of development work in the context of continuing social change. Drawing from the previous chapters it argues that there is a set of distinctive and important values and methods that are unique to development work in advanced Western societies. We return to our argument that development workers are uniquely located on the boundary between state and civil society. As such they are located at a space of acute social contradictions and this has an important impact on their role. The implications for the education, training and continuing professional development of development workers is explored, together with the implications for their roles as advocates in relation to community governance policies, present and future.

In summary, then, the following chapters provide a theoretical framework for understanding the dilemmas facing development workers, drawing on life history interviews to reveal who these workers are, where they come from and what values and capacities they bring to their work. They also provide detailed case studies of the kinds of ethical challenges involved in this kind of work, including the challenges posed by the contradictions inherent to government policies, together with strategies for addressing these, holding on to professional values, while pursuing agendas for social justice and social solidarity.

Part One
Context, role and person

TWO

The public sphere as dilemmatic space

As was argued in the introduction, development work occurs across the terrain at the interface between the state and civil society, at the point where representative and participatory democracy meet. Perhaps more than any other part of life this terrain acts as an incubator for politics – it is the site from which many social movements spring, where local activists and politicians develop, where struggles for social justice grow and decline and where inter-communal conflicts are generated. It is therefore, above all, a public sphere, a place where public purposes and values are continually contested.

Ways of thinking about the relationship between government, the state and this public sphere have changed over time. Marxist, conservative and liberal perspectives, for example, offer very different pictures of the relationship between government and the state, or between the state and civil society. The picture has recently become further complicated as the concept of *governance* appears to have replaced the less fashionable notion of government and the idea of the 'public sphere' as opposed to the 'private sphere' appears to have been undermined and attacked. In this chapter we examine the historical evolution of some of these debates and the way in which they set the context for current attempts to grasp the nature of these relationships in a world that is far more fluid, diverse and uncertain than when the practice of community development began approximately a century ago.

Contradictions of the state

Since the start of the 20th century those engaged in fighting injustice have perceived the role of government and the state in a variety of different ways. For Marxists, the state had to be understood in the context of the wider social relations of capitalist society (Miliband, 1969). In other words, the state (including public administration) could not be divorced from class relations and class interests. The state has been considered in its largely coercive dimensions, as an instrument of repression. Later the role of the state in reproducing class relations through functions such as education, urban design and social welfare became more widely recognised. From this perspective there were real limits to the extent to which the state, even in its 'softer', more welfarist forms, could ever be an effective instrument for resolving social inequalities under capitalism. Those influenced by Marxist ideas also differed in their understanding of the nature of transformatory forces in society, with Leninists emphasising the central role of the party in achieving social change, particularly through struggles in the workplace, while libertarian socialists and anarchists emphasised the self-organisation of the people not only in the workplace but in the family and community.

The Italian Marxist, Gramsci (1971), recognised that the dominance of class elites was not simply something which was occasionally contested at revolutionary conjunctures but was, in subtle and often hidden ways, contested all of the time and in all spheres of society – in culture, the classroom and the family as much as in the workplace. What he called the 'hegemony of the powerful' was always a contested hegemony. And people's consciousness was always a contested consciousness. Whereas some (overly orthodox) Marxists tended to see the human mind as a blank sheet which was either inscribed on by the dominant class or by the revolutionary party, Gramsci saw human consciousness as fundamentally contradictory, a balance of ideological forces, some passive and uncritical, others creative and emancipatory. In this sense, like Freud, but for different reasons, he saw the psyche as riven by conflicts, fundamentally contested.

Gramsci's influence on generations of postwar leftists in Europe was considerable. His way of thinking seemed to provide a space for thinking about political activism which did not simply have to wait for the arrival of the revolutionary moment, an approach to politics which recognised that the battle for ideas and for different ways of organising human life was potentially being fought out in every home, classroom and community group all the time. His understanding of the differences between political society and civil society also meant that he provided the space for less monolithic conceptions of society to emerge. This was important because in postwar Britain, at least, a new kind of state was emerging, one that looked less simply like an instrument of domination but which provided social security, free and comprehensive healthcare, social housing, retirement pensions and social care. Offe (1984) suggested that this new state seemed to be a thoroughly contradictory formation. On the one hand it had helped secure the dominance of capitalism in the postwar settlement in Western Europe but it had only been able to do so by making significant concessions to the workers and their organisations expressed in welfarism, Keynesian full employment and corporatist models of bargaining in political and economic society. In other words, the new state seemed to look both ways, it was an instrument of both ruling class domination and of labour movement emancipation. And it was this contradictory nature that appeared to open up a new site for struggle particularly in terms of what became known as the 'reproductive' role of the state – that is, its role in reproducing class relations through the family, education, welfare and so on.

Perhaps working for the state as a teacher, nurse or social worker did not necessarily mean that you were simply an instrument of control over recalcitrant schoolchildren, awkward patients or the disaffected poor. Perhaps one's role was more complicated, combining elements of control with elements of care or even possibilities for addressing social injustice. This idea became captured in the publication *In and Against the State* written by a network of UK activists and academics in the 1970s (London Edinburgh Weekend Return Group, 1980). As its title suggests, perhaps it was possible to undertake progressive work in and for the state while also being mindful of its oppressive possibilities and hence, at times, the need to take a stand against it. While democratic government was still a necessary way of legitimising the controlling and disciplining dimensions of the state, democracy itself could clearly be a means of political empowerment as progressive social democratic governments had been installed in so many Western European countries by the 1970s.

However, by this time a new form of politics had appeared on the global stage. In the South, liberation struggles against the last vestiges of colonial rule were taking place across the African continent and in South East Asia. In the West, the mobilisations of new social movements around gender, sexuality and other identities, the re-emergence of the Civil Rights Movement in the US, the development of student movements and new forms of direct action such as squatting also raised challenges about the nature of democracy. Alongside traditional notions of representative democracy more participatory forms of democracy, which emphasised collective control rather than representation, took hold. This, coupled with the realisation that civil society had a certain autonomy from the state, led to a growing interest in extending the possibilities of democratic participation through involvement in housing, childcare and other cooperatives and collectives. Soon political theorists were pushing for the expansion of democratic governance to new areas of life (Pateman, 1970), small towns and neighbourhoods (Barber, 1984). By the 1980s the practice of extended democracy was beginning to influence the development of 'service user movements', particularly in the field of health and social care. Service users, who had been traditionally excluded from the decision-making processes of professionals and the institutions in which they worked, began to demand the right to a voice in the design and delivery of the services that affected them (East London Claimants Union, 1973; Durkin and Douieb, 1975; Miller and Rein, 1975).

Finally, it is worth adding that the tide of 'democratic renewal' washed up on the shores of civil society itself as it became increasingly apparent that many so-called 'community organisations' were themselves often unaccountable, self-selected local elites, including organisations and groups criticised within the Women's Liberation Movement for practicing the 'tyranny of structurelessness' (Freeman, 1970). These ideas and practices of radical or extended democracy were current in the West for much of the late 20th century and while they have been pushed back by the advance of neoliberal modernisation processes we can see their continuing appearance in areas such as South America, particularly in the citizens' initiatives in Brazil and Argentina, as well as in recent global mobilisations such as those around the World Social Forum.

The liberal state

Classical liberalism

While in Western Europe welfarist and corporatist models of the state were emerging after the Second World War, this was not the case in the US. More minimal models of state provision continued to dominate there, and the comparative weakness of labour movement organisations meant that the state had little need to incorporate these interests in its decision-making apparatus. Traditionally, the US had a strong civil society and as a consequence 'interest group politics' tended to provide the energy that more structurally based conflicts offered in Western Europe. In the US this became associated with the concept of pluralism and pluralistic models of central and local state formation (Dahl, 1967). Pluralistic models saw the state as being free from capture by any one dominant group; rather, these approaches saw civil society almost along the lines of a marketplace for group interests, in which groups competed to get their interests onto the agenda while the state manoeuvred to gain itself a little autonomy by co-opting one group here, excluding another group there and forging a temporary alliance with another group over there. From this perspective the state was seen primarily as an intermediary, as a body that attempted to forge some notion of the public good from an assortment of competing particularisms (models that were, of course, challenged by the Civil Rights Movement, raising fundamental questions about the realities of North American democracy, as then practised). At its best the state was seen by pluralists as a reasoned actor, committed to impartiality and to a proceduralist set of ethics (du Gay, 2000).

Radical pluralism

As previously noted, by the 1970s a further wave of change was sweeping across democratic states in the West. Prevailing hierarchical modes of organising production (often termed 'Fordism') had been thrown into question by the OPEC oil crisis in 1973 (a crisis which was itself the symptom rather than cause of the economic crises of the 1970s). Traditional hierarchical models of authority in civil society were being challenged by new social movements built around the identities of gender, 'race' and sexuality. Meanwhile, in the West at least, and particularly by the 1980s, traditional structural conflicts based on class conflict seemed to be declining. While inequalities continued, particularly in Anglo-American variants of capitalism, the major redistributive inequalities increasingly appeared to become mapped onto North/South relations, that is, in terms of relations between developed and developing countries. Some began to argue that in advanced Western societies a 'politics of recognition' was emerging alongside a 'politics of redistribution' (Fraser, 1995). Civil society now seemed to be populated by new groups, organised not so much around interests but around identities, groups that sought not so much a greater slice of the cake (although many did challenge forms of inequality that impinged on the life of that group) as to challenge the cultural assumptions and social arrangements of the society in which they lived. Honneth (1995) yoked Marshall's earlier (1950) model of citizenship on to his own concept of struggles for recognition to argue that all of these groups were ultimately engaged in a struggle with the state, both to extend existing legal rights to new groups and to extend the penetration of these rights in economic, social, civil and political spheres.

There was a paradox about this new development. While on the one hand it brought new political actors on to the stage – women, gays and lesbians, Afro-Caribbeans, Latinos, people with disabilities and so on – on the other it introduced new lines of fracture within those who sought to oppose the oppressive practices of the state or the hegemony of ruling elites. These were fractures that could easily be exacerbated either as the unintended outcome of government policies (Cain and Yuval-Davis, 1990) or as the direct consequence of 'divide and rule' tactics. The pluralism of competing interest groups was being replaced by the more radical pluralism of identity-based politics, where the stakes were not just 'who gets what' but 'what kinds of social relations are we to live our lives by?'.

The significant nature of the changes taking place became even more pronounced with the onset of increased globalisation and the pressures of first economic, then political and environmental migration. Many Western democracies became increasingly multicultural, cities like London and Sydney containing over 100 official language groups. Struggles over resources between established and migrant groups and between the migrant groups themselves became overlaid by cultural and other differences, often leading to bitter and violent conflicts.

The idea of the state as an impartial mediator, coolly and rationally interposing itself between the demands of these different groups, became increasingly evidently challenged. The concepts of liberal pluralism were developed before the full flowering of what was to become known as 'identity-based' politics in which group identities such as those based around gender, sexuality, faith, ethnicity and so on were seen as giving rise to deeper and more entrenched solidarities than those based simply on mutual interest. In opposing traditional liberal models Mouffe (1993, p 113) insisted that 'politics in a modern democracy must accept division and conflict as unavoidable, and the reconciliation of rival claims and conflicting interests can only be partial and provisional'. This 'agonistic' concept of politics as struggle was also present in the work of Arendt. Speaking of Arendt, Honig noted 'she theorises a practice that is disruptive, agonistic, and, most importantly, never over' (Honig, 1993, p 9).

The key changes in traditional forms of conflict in Western democracies such as Britain and the US accompany other forms of what some call de-traditionalisation. According to Beck (1992), Bauman (1993) and others, the accelerated pace of modernity pushes all societies and their citizens towards intensified forms of destructive innovation and adaptation. All of us are forced into a world of increasing social complexity in which the stable anchors of tradition are loosened. The taken-for-granted loyalties of the past become challenged, and with this the challenge of finding satisfactory values which can act as a guide in private and public life becomes ever more daunting. This new and complex world poses a challenge to our moral and ethical capacities that were previously held more firmly within the embrace of unquestioned and simple loyalties to one's group. Today, increasingly, we belong to many different groups. Alongside the belongingness to class and nation we become aware of new group affiliations based on the largely ascribed but also partly chosen affinities of gender, ethnicity, sexuality, place and culture. Moreover, changes in the social relations of production and consumption generate a range of new occupational and lifestyle identities. Today's citizen belongs to multiple groups and in the course of a week their many different identities become salient according to the social relations they engage in. These identities pull us this way and that, sometimes, as Bauman (1993) puts it, 'one praising what the other condemns'. Tradition shelters us from responsibility. We do not have to think too much. We act in certain ways because 'people like us' do that kind of thing. In contrast, to cite Bauman again, modernity condemns us to freedom, condemns us to having to think.

Ambivalence and government

All theories of the state and government are based on some kind of view of human nature. For example, Marxism had a very different view of the human being to classical liberalism. Most variants of Marxism shared the view that our social being was manifest primarily not in discourse but in practice, that is, in the everyday actions and taken-for-granted routines of the home, neighbourhood and workplace. More recently this view has found expression in Bourdieu's (1977) concept of 'habitus', a concept he uses to refer to the milieux in which we are all embedded and which predispose us towards certain ways of thinking and feeling. But the concept of human nature of much mainstream political theory, particularly some of its liberal variants, is tacit rather than explicit. Indeed it has been one of the tasks of feminist political theory to demonstrate the way in which classical liberal theory carried with it an often disguised view of the human as a rational and autonomous being (Yeatman, 2007).

We argue that it is important to make our views about the human subject explicit in this book. One idea that we develop is that humans have an ambivalent relationship to their own flourishing. By ambivalence we mean the coexistence of opposing feelings. How is it possible to have mixed or opposing feelings about one's own development?

Our starting point is the concept of human powers or capacities. This idea has many antecedents. It is present in Marx's notion of the good society being one in which human powers could freely develop rather than assuming the alienated form of the commodity or other reified 'things'. It is also present in the work of the paediatrician and psychoanalyst Winnicott (1976), who saw human development in terms of the realisation of such capacities. One of the critiques of capitalist societies, including less avowedly capitalist societies such as China, is that they have privileged the development of some capacities, particularly technical capacities, at the expense of others such as our ethical, relational and spiritual ones (Hoggett, 2001). A complete view of the human subject would see all of these capacities as essential to full human subjecthood. The task is to develop political and social relationships that can enable these capacities to flourish. This perspective is not dissimilar to that recently put forward by Nussbaum (2000; 2001, pp 224-9), who attempts to outline a list of central human capabilities which would have universal application. For Nussbaum these include bodily integrity, imagination and thought, practical reason, affiliation and play, emotion, bodily health, life, senses, living with other species and control over one's environment. According to Nussbaum, a just society would provide for such capabilities. While sympathetic to her project, Sen (2002) is critical of her approach for being overly specific and therefore subject to criticism by those who are more culturally relativist. We feel that our approach avoids this criticism by focusing on capacities rather than more specific capabilities. As we use it, the concept of capacity (a concept we explore in more detail in subsequent chapters) draws attention to what is potentially realisable rather than towards fixed human attributes. A good society would be a society in which technical, emotional and ethical capacities would be equally valued and in which social arrangements would make it possible for them to flourish in a balanced way.

We suggest that there is an added twist to this. As human beings we are ambivalent about our own flourishing and the flourishing of others. Long ago Thomas Hobbes put forward a very different view of the human being, one that emphasised the importance of egoism, fear and envy. As Alford (1992) points out, the desire for power pictured by Hobbes has many parallels with Hegel's notion of the desire for recognition, and the master/slave dialectic that flows from this. For Marx, this egoistical struggle is the consequence of private property and the alienation of human powers in money and commodities. As Marx puts it, 'each tries to establish over the other an *alien power*, so as to thereby find satisfaction of his own selfish need ... his neediness grows as the power of money increases' (Marx, 1970, p 147; emphasis added). Marx's appropriation of Hegel therefore underscores his theory of alienation. The same theme, concerning the alienation of human powers, resurfaces in French existentialist thought, but here alienation is construed as both inherent to human nature *and* the outcome of class society. In a similar way, Freud saw life dominated by two powerful forces, of love and hate, connection and disconnection, association and fragmentation, which had a profound influence on social life but which were also strongly influenced by social life.

Irrespective of whether we see the negative capacities of human beings as inherent to their nature or as a product of the social arrangements through which they live, it is clear that negative emotions such as hate, destructiveness, fear and envy have played a powerful role in most, if not all, societies, past and present. A good society is therefore one that, while bringing out the best in us, is also able to inhibit, ameliorate or transform the worst in us. And this enables us to deepen our understanding of government. At its best, good government enables us to become more civilised beings. As Plato put it, government is as much about soulcraft as it is about statecraft. And given that no society has so far been created which is not based on relations of domination and subordination, the distinction between the state as an instrument of control and the state as a means of managing our ambivalent relation to life and to others is a complex and contradictory one.

One implication of this perspective is that the relationships between citizens and governments are marked by ambivalence. We may find it difficult to face up to and accept our negative emotions and impulses. We are prone to disown them and seek others to blame for them. The fears that citizens may have about madness, violence, their own frailties and vulnerabilities and so on may be easily denied so that the government is blamed for not doing enough about these things. When government acts, citizens then often resent the actions taken, and it becomes a convenient whipping horse for our own collective irresponsibility and failure. So we believe that something must be done to improve services to those with mental ill health, asylum seekers or homeless people, but when community initiatives are implemented to tackle these issues local residents often object to the location of such facilities in the neighbourhood. We tend to forget that citizens, including ourselves, are capable of being 'ugly citizens' who pursue selfish agendas, are fearful of listening to the views of others that seem strange or different and who believe their own grievances are always justified. But grievances are not always justified, particularly when they are aimed, as in racism, at target groups who are relatively weak and defenceless. The social inequalities of class society compound this ambivalence. As a recent publication of activists and academics put it, 'a society that makes large numbers of its citizens feel that they are looked down on will inevitably incur the costs of people's antisocial reactions' (Compass, 2006, p 24).

Complexity of the public sphere

The public sphere therefore needs to be considered from several different perspectives if the full complexity of working in this sphere is to be appreciated. It includes government, the apparatus of the state and civil society, indeed all those institutions, organisations and associations which populate that territory between the two private spheres of our intimate relations and family life on the one hand, and what we think of as the 'private sector' (companies, firms, etc) on the other. But even this is not a hard and fast distinction. One of the impacts of feminist and other movements has been to push back the frontiers of what might be considered 'private' in our intimate relations so that, for example, abusive practices in families have become a legitimate territory for public intervention. Similarly, with the spread of powerful and secretive private equity firms a number of commentators have argued that the value of 'public companies' with accountable shareholders, whose operations are governed by company law and so on, needs to be appreciated before it is too late (Hutton, 1999). Given these provisos we nevertheless suggest that the definition of the public sphere that we have offered provides a useful working definition of an area of life which should be open, to varying degrees, to public scrutiny, debate and accountability. The two essential characteristics of the public sphere are therefore transparency and contestability. All actors within the public sphere should be inherently accountable because the public sphere is a sphere of public (as opposed to private) concern. Of course it is already linked to and affected by, rather than sealed off from, the operations of the market. To reduce the size of this sphere, for example by privatising public organisations, by restricting freedom of information or by handing public institutions over to management by self-selected elites, is to reduce the territory where the public enjoys a legitimate concern by making action opaque rather than transparent and potentially visible. Secondly, the public sphere is contestable. Because actions, decisions, policies and procedures are potentially visible, citizens are provided with the basis for contesting them, for criticising them or for posing alternatives. It follows that the public sphere is also the sphere of public discourse, that part of society in which collective values and purposes can be expressed, argued about and developed. This is in fact what becomes defined as 'politics', and is the territory where political parties, social movements and community organisations operate. Again, to the extent that the public sphere is reduced in size or scope, the sphere of democratic politics is similarly reduced.

We have seen that powerful classes and elites influence the structure, agenda and practices of the public sphere (often by attempting to restrict its transparency and contestability) but that this hegemony is not monolithic. The public institutions of welfare societies express subaltern as well as elite interests, they provide programmes and offer services that ordinary citizens often fight to preserve. We have also argued that in advanced Western democracies power has become increasingly dispersed, traditional forms of interest group politics have become overlaid by new and powerful group identities, some of which correspond to what have become known as the new social movements. But this has also become the site for new social divisions and tensions, particularly along ethnic lines. Finally we have suggested that relations between citizens on the one hand, and governments and state institutions on the other, are marked by ambivalence, that the latter often become recipients of the alienated powers of the former, as if we can neither live happily with too much government nor live happily without it. We want the state to intervene more and then we resent it when it does; we want the state to keep its distance and then we blame it for abrogating its responsibilities. The point is that this is not just about the way in which the state goes about its work, although it often does this in a clumsy and inept manner. The point we are trying to make is that the state and its street-level officials cannot but help get it wrong, too often, because this is part of the dynamic of ambivalence – part of continuing struggles to balance the competing demands and desires of those in need of services with the limits imposed as a result of wider underlying power structures.

Dilemmatic space

Ethics is concerned with the rules, standards, feelings and beliefs that govern the way in which we make judgements about right and wrong, good and bad. Traditionally, debates on ethics tended to focus around two different approaches. Kantian approaches (based on the theoretical framework developed by the 18th-century philosopher, Immanuel Kant) start from the view that we can share a universalist set of norms, based on the principle of respect for all people. In summary, this implies that we should all behave, in every situation, in ways that 'treat humanity, whether in your own person or that of any other, never solely as a means but always as an end' (Kant, 1964, quoted in Banks, 2006, p 29). In other words, respect for others, including the client/service user, must always come first. Such a view has, of course, featured in principles and codes of professional ethics, such as principles that have been key to professional social work and youth work.

In practice, however, this type of approach has also had its critics. There are limits to the extent to which each individual can always come first, for example, just as there are limits to the extent to which a Kantian approach might address issues of structural inequality, such as racism and sexism. Social considerations are also involved here. This brings the discussion to the next type of approach, utilitarian, based on the principle that the right action is that which produces the greatest balance of good (the greatest 'utility') for the greatest number of people. In practice, utilitarian approaches have also been influential, for example, in debates on how to prioritise needs in the allocation of public services. Professionals do make judgements that take account of such considerations – how to ensure the most effective use of scarce resources, to have the most impact on the greatest number of those who need them. As Banks points out, however, utilitarian approaches are also, ultimately, unsatisfactory (Banks, 2006). As she explains, by themselves they do not tell us whose good we should promote nor how we decide conflicts between other principles (such as principles of justice and equity). There are still issues of judgement to be resolved.

More recently a range of other approaches have been developed, including radical approaches, emphasising that respect for human beings also involves issues of justice and equality, with collective as well as individual empowerment (Banks, 2006), an approach with considerable relevance for community development workers. Rather than explore these differing approaches in detail, the point to emphasise here is simply this: that far from providing a clear set of rules, the study of ethics offers differing and potentially competing frameworks for the exercise of judgement as to the right course of action in any particular set of circumstances.

It is commonplace nowadays to make a distinction between what Banks (2004) describes as impartialist and partialist approaches to ethics. The former stress the importance of universal principles, the idea being that the person can deduce ethical courses of action from these abstract standards. Examples of such principles would include the concept of equality and social justice or the idea that all people are worthy of being treated with equal respect. Such impartialist approaches tended to dominate social policy over much of the last century but have recently come under sustained criticism from feminist and postmodernist critics. These critics have argued that far from being universal such principles often conceal a particular (typically white, male and colonial) perspective. Take liberalism's advocacy of individual freedom, critics have argued that this assumes the existence of a rational, autonomous, individual agent with the right and the ability to make choices, but how does this apply to cultures which put the group before the individual and cannot conceive of the individual except as one subordinate element within a complex web of inter-relationships? Partialist approaches to ethics stress the importance of context. They argue that, for example, what may constitute equal treatment in individualist New York may not be seen as equal treatment in collectivist Cameroon. They also stress that the ethical actor is not some abstract individual but a person rooted in a web of relationships, with their own feelings, dispositions and responsibilities. If a young single man decides to give up his good job and go and do voluntary work in Africa we may commend his ethical behaviour, but if a father suddenly abandons his partner and children to do the same thing we may be less certain about how to respond.

Professions such as youth and community work and social work do, of course, have their own ethical codes. These provide some guidance for action. Typically, these codes combine differing approaches to ethics (with Kantian-type respect for the value of individual clients/young people, for example, and the need to protect and promote their rights, together with an emphasis on the need to develop anti-oppressive and anti-discriminatory practice). As Banks has also demonstrated, there are differences between professional codes as these have been developed in different countries (Banks, 2004), and codes of ethics can and do vary over time. By definition, professional codes of ethics are partial, rather than absolute, in terms of the guidance that they can offer, and professionals need to use their judgement to apply them in particular sets of circumstances.

In this book we argue that principles are vital for a development worker to have, but they are also insufficient. In Chapter Five we show how these principles are often rooted in development workers' earlier life experiences, and therefore not some learned 'add on' but a part of who they are. These principles are therefore the foundation of the passionate commitment of many development workers to what they do. But while such principles can provide guidance, they only provide certainty for the misguided. Because development work occurs in that contested space between state and civil society, and because the interest and identity groups that populate socially diverse civil societies have conflicting values, rules and needs there is no unambiguous terrain on which one's principles can be put to work. Risk, uncertainty and ambiguity are the development worker's constant companion and in this book we argue that workers need the equipment (personal and social resources) to operate in a principled way in such settings. In other words, rather than seeing them as opposing alternatives we argue that both impartialist and partialist perspectives are equally relevant to development workers who, nevertheless, have the further burden of managing the tension between these two very different approaches in their own practice.

The public sphere is central to the development of our ethical capacities. It is in this sphere that different value systems embrace and collide and different pictures of the good society are expressed, debated and developed. A truly democratic politics welcomes argument and conflict about matters of public concern at all levels of life and recognises that the more that ordinary citizens are involved (even vicariously) the more their own values and principles are tested.

As argued earlier, liberal democracies look two ways. They express gains made and rights won by subaltern classes and groups and yet at the same time provide legitimation for the continuation of a class-based society in which inequality is built into the very structure of social relations. Even within the parameters set by class societies, the core values of liberalism – liberty, equality and fraternity – are ultimately incommensurable. At a certain point more equality necessarily entails less liberty, particularly in the economic sphere, and similarly more liberty (personal freedoms) entails less fraternity (collective solidarities). Conservative, centrist and social democratic parties attach differential emphasis to such values and in doing so necessarily engage in a certain blindness to the values they neglect. Marris and Rein put it thus:

> Confronted by the dilemmas of social choice, reform does not seem most characteristically to search for balance. Instead, it takes up each of the incompatible principles in turn, and campaigns for it as if no sacrifice of its alternative were entailed. And this seemingly irrational refusal to come to terms with the fundamental dilemma may, after all, be more productive than accommodation. By repudiating whatever balance has been struck, it continually challenges society to explore new ways of meeting the problem. (Marris and Rein, 1972, p 233)

From this perspective, conflict, impassioned and ongoing, is an essential condition for vitality in public life. But, and this is crucial for our thinking, it also follows that the public sphere (which includes the organised apparatus of government) expresses these conflictual purposes. And while different political projects emphasise different values, those that they suppress inevitably return to haunt the political system, typically returning at the level at which policy is implemented. As Lipsky noted, 'a typical mechanism for legislative conflict resolution is to pass on intractable conflicts for resolution (or continued irresolution) at the administrative level' (Lipsky, 1980, p 41). As a consequence, it is often at the level of 'operations' that unresolved value conflicts are most sharply enacted, public officials and local representatives finding themselves 'living out' rather than 'acting on' the contradictions of the complex and diverse society in which they live.

It is possible to see a similar perspective in Jessop's recent reflections on 'the coordination problem', that is, do markets' hierarchies or networks provide the most effective basis for organising productive activities (including those of government)? Jessop's conclusion is that failure is inherent to all modes of coordination and yet policy actors must proceed as if success were possible (Jessop, 2003). Marris and Rein, and Jessop all indicate that when faced with value dilemmas, human actors appear to adopt a one-eyed approach and, moreover, that this may be the most effective way to proceed, even if it is done (as Jessop advocates) with a necessary touch of irony. But then this brings us to the nature of ethical conflicts and dilemmas and the stance that human actors take towards them.

Ours is a complex world, one still riven by injustices but where strategies to work towards solutions to such injustices are often hard to agree. Developing such strategies to tackle these fundamental problems – to make a real difference in the here and now while having an eye to longer-term social transformation – is immensely difficult. Moreover, it is a world in which differences such as culture, religion and gender easily become the basis for new social divisions, dividing one group against another. In this world simple distinctions between right and wrong become increasingly hard to sustain for what may seem just for one group is seen as unjust by another. But it is also a world in which the stakes are increasingly high. Given the power of military technologies, the might of multinational companies and global finance, we now live in a world in which the destructive potential of our present-day social arrangements finds persistent expression in avoidable famine, genocide and ethnic cleansing and the growing catastrophe of global warming. Nor are Western democracies any longer immune to such destructive consequences as globalisation threatens established labour markets and ways of life, undermines postwar welfare arrangements and weakens the social fabrics of urban and rural communities alike. Paradoxically then, the more vital politics becomes the more difficult it is to know the right course of action and this is as true for an elected political leader as it is for a local activist or development worker engaged in the implementation of a public programme.

Our group loyalties, to our class, gender, nation, ethnic community and so on, and the commitments that accompany them, are often in tension. Part of the 'project of the self' becomes the negotiation of such tensions, tensions that find expression in the dilemmas of everyday life. According to Honig (1996), we live in 'dilemmatic space', a space in which there is no longer any obvious right thing to do. We feel torn, between conflicting 'pulls', so that we often think to ourselves 'well on the one hand … but then on the other…'. In such ambiguous settings it may be tempting to retreat into a world of certainty, one where principles become a rigid dogma. Even if it is clear to us what we *must* do we can still feel torn because a residual feeling remains that perhaps it is not the thing we *should* be doing. In such situations moral philosophers such as Williams (1973, 1981) suggest that all we can do is 'act for the best'.

This suggestion has particular relevance for those engaged in development work. But, if we remain open to the complexity of things, in acting for the best we may still be beset by anxiety because we may feel that the course of action we have rejected may turn out to have been the right one after all. As we shall see in Chapter Six, development workers are constantly faced with risk and the possibility of failure, particularly failure to live up to their own values and standards. And after the course of action has been concluded the agent typically experiences lingering feelings of doubt, regret and sometimes guilt. For some people this complexity may become incapacitating, leading to passivity and a feeling of impotence. To be aware of opposing perspectives, to have the capacity to take the standpoint of the other, may offer a form of integrity but at the price of agonising indecision – the opposite problem to the dogmatist. To recognise complexity and yet still retain the capacity for action requires considerable intellectual and emotional resources from the individuals and groups concerned. It requires a new kind of politics, one where social movements can act without the consolation of feeling that they necessarily have all the right on their side. The alternative is to run the risk of a victory that simply replaces one form of domination by another. It is this reflexive activism (King, 2006) that is one of the central themes for exploration in this book.

THREE

The nature of development work

This chapter begins with an account of community development that defines it as a form of state intervention. While the overall focus is wider than community development per se, including a wider range of professionals with a 'development' brief, the history of community development has relevance for a critical understanding of the roots and inherent tensions of public policies towards community engagement and community capacity building. As the chapter demonstrates, community development approaches have been applied, and misapplied, in varying ways, over time.

Having explored some of the competing definitions of community development, the chapter then considers the relationship between this and collective action within civil society before exploring the tension between the potential contribution of community development to a more just and equal society and its complex and often contradictory roles in the current context. Community development has long been considered an elusive and contested concept, its purpose difficult to define even by those directly involved in its practice. Indeed, Hoatson (2003, p 23) describes any generalisation as a 'dangerous practice'. Community development sits on the unstable boundary between state and civil society, both reflecting and seeking to change those relationships (Mayo and Craig, 1995). It embodies values inimical to the dominant commodity relationships of the market that influence our perception of the public sphere and the meaning attributed to development. Its practice is situational and contextual. In Britain it has recently undergone another process of re-branding and is now more frequently referred to as 'community engagement', 'community cohesion' or more loosely still to a variety of roles associated with combating 'social exclusion'. Such shifts have expanded the scope of 'development', importing the process into the roles of a multitude of welfare professionals, but also diluted the nature of development and the qualities, skills and knowledge necessary to successfully undertake it (Miller, 2004).

As with other professional practices, community development has a history from which has emerged a set of espoused values and a body of knowledge, practices and philosophy (Mayo and Robertson, 2003). Yet these are insufficiently robust, frequently contested and cannot be contained within a regulatory professional body in such a way as to be able to promote and protect a particular position. Further, indeterminate role boundaries create opportunities for practitioners to influence the way development is defined by allowing their own personal identities and values to construct the primary task. Although often presented as a force for social change the scope for this is limited and the scale of community development's achievements are influenced by the strength of other more powerful forces, such as social movements, political parties, trade unions and the economy. In other words, it is dependent on what is politically feasible.

In Britain the state, at both central and local level, has been the primary source of funding for community development, both in the direct funding of posts and projects but also indirect funding via support to voluntary and community sector organisations, where many community development practitioners are employed. Increasingly, such funding is time-limited and tied to specific government programmes, initiatives and targets.

Conflicting identities

Community development practitioners confront dilemmas similar to other colleagues within the public sphere. They are, for example, just as likely to feel a strong sense of identity with a professional public service role (Hoggett, Beedell, Jimenez, Mayo and Miller, 2006). There is also the shared identity of public service employee and trade union member. However, there is some ambiguity in the attachment to professionalism since running through the veins of community development is a strong association with an anti-professional position, perhaps more so than in other welfare occupations. Unlike other public service workers, community development practitioners are trained, accredited and usually employed by the state to take up a role that can bring them into conflict with their employer. Since the state is more often than not the employer in question this experience is not comparable with other worker–employer disputes in which employees challenge some enterprise-specific and narrow interest. Rather, what is being questioned is the authority of the state itself, standing at the pinnacle of society, as *the* authoritative voice. Individual line managers and elected representatives can appear to embody the full legitimising weight of state authority in a demand for acquiescence to hierarchical requirements. Yet if the relationship between the practitioner and employer is a source of tension then so too is the relationship between the practitioner and the constituency with whom they work. For as we shall see in Chapter Seven, very often it is the practitioner who is perceived to be an authority, even though they may not feel like one. The practitioner is often in the paradoxical position of challenging but also representing 'the authorities', while also being someone who works to enable others to take up their own authority (Hoggett, Mayo and Miller, 2006). Yet it is an authority that comes with no statutory powers of enforcement. It is therefore a relationship in which a disarmed agent of authority meets with the citizen to authorise the latter, and the outcome is indeterminate.

Beyond such identities embodied within the formal role are those that practitioners bring that are more personal. Here we might think of the identity as an activist committed to social justice and equity, a citizen who favours public provision over the marketplace, a democrat committed to the extension of democratic values, practices and dialogue, a cosmopolitan who values the added richness and stimulation of a society that embraces diversity, or someone who has personally experienced social disadvantage that has had life-shaping consequences. Practitioners might also identify strongly with a class, ethnicity or gender and seek to focus work around such politics. In other words, these and other identities and the associated emotions are not simply personal self-expressions but can become embedded within their professional practice. They can also be part of the sometimes unspoken expectations of employers, in addition to formal education and professional qualification requirements. Employers seek to recruit those with such strong identities in order that they might be used and exploited as experiential points of contact with those who are the objects of professional practice. The application of such emotional labour with the passion and enthusiasms that tend to flow from such identities is considered essential to the effective performance of the professional role. However, the consequences of doing so are not always equally valued and the boundary between practitioner subjectivities and the professional role is uncertain and a place of constant (re)-negotiation.

The diverse nature of practitioners' identities reflects the growing social diversity of Western-type democracies such as Britain. As noted in Chapter One, this social diversity also adds complexity to our ethical lives, as different cultures are sometimes governed by very different principles, customs and ways of living. For the development practitioner this can pose difficult ethical challenges as the following example shows.

A community empowerment network (CEN) is developed for an area in a large city with a very diverse array of communities from different parts of Africa. A number of places are set aside on the CEN for members of these black and minority ethnic (BME) groups in particular, their role being to ensure that as many different voices as possible are heard from their respective communities. However, after the CEN has been established for a while it becomes clear to some in the CEN team that the members of these BME groups see themselves as representatives rather than facilitators – speaking for their communities rather than acting as a conduit to them. There is an anxiety that women, younger people and members of minority groups and faiths may not be properly included. Members of the CEN team are divided about whether and how to challenge these individuals; many are senior members of their own communities. Matters are made more complex by the fact that the CEN team is largely young and white and there is an anxiety that any challenge to the BME members may be met by accusations of racism.

Community development and community engagement as interventions by the state

Community development can be thought of as one of a number of intervention strategies available to government in response to perceived community problems. Until recently, as it has grown in significance, community development was a relatively marginal strategy and practitioners were under-resourced and located on the fringes of public service organisations. During the previous decade this has changed, both in Britain and elsewhere, as community development principles, values and methods have come to be recognised and have featured prominently in major new policy initiatives (Gilchrist, 2003). They have been added to the toolkits of a variety of public service professionals who are now expected to adopt a community orientation in their practice, engage in 'capacity building', build collaborative relationships with other stakeholders and develop joined-up policy interventions, while the role and status of community development specialists has likewise expanded (Taylor, 2003).

In principle, a community development strategy could be applied to all communities equally as part of the normal way of managing state–civil society dynamics and facilitating good inter-community relationships in a diverse society. In practice such interventions have been targeted, small-scale, time-restricted and focused on those defined as disadvantaged economically, socially, materially, culturally or otherwise lacking in influence or excluded from the mainstream. The prioritising of disadvantaged or excluded communities, which may be defined spatially, by interest or shared values, is justified on the grounds that such conditions are inimical to a developed social democracy. The presence of such conditions both detracts from the image of an economically prosperous, inclusive and just society and ultimately poses a threat to social order. Community development is a demonstration of concern that such conditions exist and for those experiencing such disadvantage, but it also represents a commitment to address the causes of disadvantage or at least ameliorate their worst consequences. Such targeted interventions are underpinned by a rationale that acknowledges the need for corrective change, sets out desired objectives and a commitment to a development strategy to 'bridge the gap' between life chances in the most deprived areas and those typical of the rest of the country at large. It is both a means to an end and an end in itself, bringing people together to solve a problem and mirroring democratic practices in diverse and complex settings.

Multiple motives are likely to be found within any single intervention, often in conflict with each other. Typically, state-led community development is driven by any combination of three key objectives. Firstly, we can speak of the management of *intra-community* tensions impacting on social cohesion and threatening disintegration arising from major social disruptions. Such threats may occur in response to some known and predictable event, such as the physical redevelopment of a neighbourhood, or have evolved over time, as with the appearance and growth of new and 'different' or 'other' social groups into an existing or 'settled' community. In such circumstances the value of community development is perceived to be its capacity to rebuild or create social networks and local community organisations, find practical ways to address a specific social problem, including the management of disaffected groups, or to identify ways for conflict transformation. Secondly, it is increasingly utilised as a method of local policy implementation by mobilising local community resources, better connecting service agencies with the people and neighbourhoods they serve, encouraging local communities to provide services that either complement or replace state and private sector services or as a way of acquiring or communicating information about local problems, concerns or attitudes. Thirdly, it is a way of enhancing or providing greater legitimacy for local democracy by increasing the levels of public participation in public issues and strengthening both direct and representative democracy. This might be done by building stronger connections between citizens, local organisations, political representatives and local political structures, increasing the capacity of civil society organisations, strengthening the sense of agency among citizens and demonstrating symbolically that the government remains connected with and concerned about community-specific issues even when unable, unwilling or unsure of how to address them directly.

Community development, however, also signals a broader concern for the common good. In other words, it can claim to represent values and processes that reflect core social democratic principles, such as mutual recognition for others and tolerance in relation to difference founded on a model of social justice and equal rights. Similarly its practice reflects an on-going process of finding an effective balance between the competing claims and limitations of both representative and direct or participant democracy. Community development then contains aspirational goals for society in general as well as a means to an end for specific communities at particular moments in time. As a professional activity it is unusual if not unique in its mandate to strengthen democratic values and capacities and to promote and extend democratic practices, in part through a process of questioning those that exist. It embodies or expresses the values of the social democratic polity even when the immediate focus is on a narrow, conservative and limited set of objectives (Shaw, 2008a).

While the quality of a society might be judged by the degree of social and economic equality (Marshall, 1963; Lister, 2004), typically of even greater concern to governments is the knowledge that extreme levels of inequality could trigger widespread social unrest. Community development as a specific type of strategic intervention can be located along a continuum of other choices open to government, including at one end that of military force, for example as in Northern Ireland (where in recent decades both community development interventions and military force were applied during periods of civil disturbances), as a way of keeping the peace, maintaining social order, or in response to profound levels of dissent. This is not to deny the potential for community development to bring about progressive social and economic change but rather to acknowledge that it stands alongside other possible options for any government faced with what it defines as a social problem requiring an organised response.

Community development is rarely considered to be the only response in relation to any community problem or even the most significant one among other policy measures. However, a community development strategy or a community-centred approach to policy more generally is increasingly considered essential if other ultimately more significant interventions are to work. In other words, communities need first to be somehow 'turned around' if they are to benefit from other opportunities as delivered through mainstream services such as education, health and social care, housing or environment. This is a 'deficit' model of community. Targeted communities are thought to be lacking – in need of more social cohesion, stronger bridging ties to the mainstream economy and more engaged in public matters. But at the same time it is often argued that they need to feel recognised, valued and able to access on an equal basis those resources commonly available to others.

The object of change or principal beneficiary of community development is the community itself or some significant element within it. The vehicle of change is collective action often in the form of the mobilisation of some formal structure such as a community group, organisation, network or alliance. It focuses on those individuals, groups, social networks and collectivities that appear to act as a focal point for the neighbourhood, faith, ethnic group or other social identity. Community development can also be of benefit to individual participants in a number of ways including, for example, gains to self-confidence, a sense of recognition or self-worth, learning practical, organisational, personal and inter-personal skills and knowledge acquisition. Individuals also gain from collective improvements to the environment, local conditions and amenities, public services or better and more effective governance arrangements including greater opportunities for community members to influence policy developments and implementation. For many the motivation for becoming involved in a local initiative is the prospect of improving personal circumstances or making the neighbourhood a better place to live. The primary objective of the development task is to focus on common interests, concerns, priorities and solutions, as defined by the community in question, and to pursue these through collective action with a view to securing benefits for all, including those who choose not to directly participate in the process. The process is underpinned by a set of core values that include a commitment to inclusivity of membership, full community representativeness in all its diversity, ensuring that all voices can be heard, transparency in relation to organisational processes and decision making, a sharing of tasks, responsibilities and roles including those of leadership, accountability to the wider community for actions taken, collaborative working with other similar communities and working within a human rights, social justice and capacities framework.

Competing discourses on 'community'

Britain has a long, albeit uneven, history stretching back to the end of the 19th century of direct intervention in disadvantaged or marginal communities by the central and local state as well as faith-based bodies, national NGOs, such as universities and charities, and increasingly international bodies, both supra-state and non-governmental agencies. Indirect interventions have come from philanthropic foundations, and others through the construction of social programmes against which they invite funding bids, and in a financially restricted market, can be powerful mechanisms in shaping the nature of interventions. During the past 40 years, however, it is the state that has been the major employer of development practitioners and the primary source of funds for voluntary and community-based organisations.

The explanation for community disadvantage, marginality or exclusion that then requires intervention is often attributed to some external source, such as economic decline, or to something internal to the community or a combination of both. As the object of policy intervention, such communities have often been conceived of as relatively homogeneous entities with locally specific values, cultures, social practices and material interests. Such characteristics can be perceived as resources to be mobilised, constraints that must be challenged either to preserve something valued that is threatened or modified in pursuit of something desirable, or absent and needing to be inserted to contribute to community well-being (Shaw, 2008a).

There are a number of powerful and competing discourses about such communities. One tradition connects it to loss and change (Young and Willmott, 1957; Seabrook, 1984) and implies that community is something that has been 'lost', such as particular values or a way of life that should be preserved even or perhaps especially when the rest of society no longer functions in these ways. Communities, such as those that were once synonymous with mining industries, can take on an almost heroic quality, as survivors against seemingly insuperable odds or tragic victims of harsh circumstances, such as economic restructuring through globalisation, but communities that nevertheless contain individual members and groups who, with support, can recover.

Another powerful discourse linked to the concept of 'cycles of deprivation' (Murray, 1984) sees such communities as pathologically dysfunctional, unable to prosper, but operating in ways that undermine other policy initiatives or block progress. Instead they are the generators and reproducers of social problems leading to damaged environments, intra-community conflict, unruly, disruptive and potentially offending children, dysfunctional families, adults disconnected from the labour market and acting as a seedbed of criminality and a drain on public resources. In other words, they represent those who can be classified as a 'burden' to society. Alternatively they represent groups for whom events have conspired to deny them equal access to opportunities or benefits shared by the majority. Without the social resources or capital to address such inequalities effectively, for themselves, such communities are perceived to be in need of community development for reasons of social justice.

A third discourse recognises that in addition to any common interests, shared values, practices or injustices, communities are also contested places, constantly in flux, constructed on fragile social relationships that can be deeply divisive and are increasingly diverse (Brent, 1997). Such diversity can mean that within any one 'community' there can be in existence a number of smaller communities holding differential identities with those surrounding them. In such circumstances to identify and access key points of entry to one community may not provide access to other communities nested within the larger one. The need for governments to focus on community cohesion was reflected in the Cantle report (2001) and the Home Office's 'Community Cohesion Pathfinder Programme' (2003-04) and subsequent report (Home Office, 2005). The Cantle Review, established to inquire into social disturbances in a number of northern British towns earlier that year, warned of growing neighbourhood polarisation, division and the absence of any inter-community communication within the same neighbourhood. Indeed, communities based on ethnicity or faith were described as occupying the same spatial territory but living in different, parallel worlds. The extent of such separation has been the subject of subsequent discussion and debate. There is, in fact, evidence of considerable neighbourliness across such community divides in many contexts, with potentially decreasing friction as and when contact between communities increases (UK Citizenship Survey, 2007). Yet public policy continues to be concerned with anxieties and moral panics about 'community cohesion', especially so since the bombings in London in July 2005 and the so-called 'War on Terror' in Britain and beyond, internationally.

While any one of these discourses on community can dominate the policy agenda at any one time it is more likely that a number of seemingly contradictory discourses will be operating simultaneously across policy fields. In part this reflects the complexity of social realities and how these are understood. It also reflects unevenness in analysis within and between various state institutions, different levels of the state, and between different explanatory frameworks. Further, community development as an effective strategy to mobilise community-based interests can be used by any level of the state, particularly by the elected representatives, as a way of influencing its relationships with other levels. For example, during the mid-1980s with the neoliberal Conservative government of Margaret Thatcher intent on diminishing the power of local government and curtailing or marketising public provision, a number of left-of-centre Labour-controlled local authorities sought to mobilise community organisations and some spoke of an alliance of trade unions, civil society organisations and local councils against central government policies. In other words 'community' was mobilised, in part through the use of public funds to support local groups, by one political grouping with a view to dislodging another, both of whom were democratically elected albeit by different constituencies and each claiming a mandate for its actions (Miller, 1996). During the early 1970s the UK Labour government of Harold Wilson, drawing on the North American anti-poverty programmes, initiated the 12 innovative Community Development Projects (CDPs) in selected authorities but ensured that government civil servants and local members of parliament (MPs) remained involved in their oversight as a way of tackling what was seen as lethargy and resistance among local authority-elected members and public servants. In other words, CDPs were tasked with shaking up some of those local authorities resistant to change during a period that central government declared as one of new opportunities and social progress (Loney, 1983).

A historically flexible and responsive strategy

The UK government first used community development after the Second World War as a strategy in its then colonies to assist it in the process of de-colonisation (Mayo, 2000). It was applied as an educational process to export a 'British model' to ensure that those countries about to secure independence would nevertheless reproduce values, political practices and institutions that mirrored those of their former colonial masters. Similar policies and some of the same development practitioners were subsequently mobilised in Britain for the (re)-building of a community 'spirit' and strengthening social networks in the postwar large-scale social housing projects and New Towns that were to accommodate working-class families uprooted from over-crowded, inadequate, neglected or war-damaged inner-city neighbourhoods. It was between the mid-1960s and the mid-1970s, however, that community development strongly emerged to offer solutions to a range of social concerns and as a response to the growth of community action and social movements demanding greater social, political and economic freedoms. Such developments in Britain were also strongly influenced by similar events in the US, most notably the Civil Rights Movement and the War on Poverty but also the emergence of women's and gay rights movements (Popple, 1995).

There were particular concerns, of which the CDPs and the long-running Urban Programme were a product, for those communities and regions facing multiple disadvantages that had been left behind by the growing affluence and social opportunities that were a consequence of postwar economic growth and the benefits of the welfare state. In the midst of such overall progress poverty was re-discovered (Abel-Smith and Townsend, 1965), housing and homelessness remained a major social problem (Coates and Silburn, 1970), a significant number of children were found to be disadvantaged in education opportunities and outcomes while illness and poor health continued to be over-concentrated in particular areas and traditional family patterns and relationships appeared to be dissolving, raising concerns about parenting, the care of dependants and the strength of social networks.

In response to this social and economic landscape, NGOs such as Shelter, Mind, Age Concern, Release and the Child Poverty Action Group (CPAG) emerged to act as advocates for the disadvantaged and to press for policy changes. Such predominantly middle-class groups were mirrored by a plethora of local neighbourhood-based groups such as tenants' associations, claimants unions and others, coming together in opposition to unwelcome and ill-conceived urban development initiatives, the management of local services and in response to a diverse range of unmet needs and both old and new social problems. Such levels of dissatisfaction meant that everything from the level and quality of public services, the decline of local shops, amenities and transport, environmental decay and redevelopment, policing, 'problem' families, social housing rents and maintenance, domestic violence, gender and 'race' inequalities, the local economy and labour market issues, to welfare benefits and minority rights, became a focus of local action and the basis for a new community group to emerge. Activists demanded access to all decisions that impacted on local communities and an extension of personal rights, choices and freedoms in relation to local state services, professional interventions and regulations, and they were occasionally supported by government policy documents such as the 1969 Skeffington Report (1969) on local planning and redevelopment. In the face of rising social problems, the failure of social policies and a sense of dislocation from the state, community development offered governments a way forward, a positive response that other state policies lacked.

Meanwhile tensions and conflict continued to persist in relation to those BME communities who had migrated to Britain after the Second World War, frequently in response to the encouragement of employers and the state, seeking to fill empty spaces in the growing economy, including those in the public sector, for example in transport and nursing. Such minority communities were increasingly inclined to build organisations to defend themselves against discrimination and abuse in both the workplace and the neighbourhood and to find their political voice (Sondhi, 1995). Other social groups, notably women but also single parents, gays and lesbians, homeless people and people with physical or mental impairments, were also coming together to speak out to better understand their situation and demand, often through direct action, an end to social, political and economic injustices (Dominelli, 1990).

As the angry voices grew louder, the tactics of pressure became more conflictual, with the local authority regularly singled out as the primary source of dissatisfaction, despite the efforts of programmes such as the CDPs to locate the problem more broadly in underlying structural factors, particularly the unfettered and socially irresponsible development of capitalism that made and then broke industrial areas, in pursuit of higher profits elsewhere (CDP Inter-Project Editorial Team, 1977). Not surprisingly, when these latter forms of criticism were developed, those involved with CDPs became subject to pressure to curb activities. Community development outcomes frequently raised awkward questions for senior managers, challenging local policy decisions and front-line professional practice across all welfare services. Further, the direct democracy typical of community action was seen to be undermining the legitimacy of locally elected councillors rather than acting as a complementary form of accountability. During the latter part of the 1970s community development continued to be one of the strategic tools adopted by local authorities, albeit with greater managerial control. With increasing pressures on funding, with the public sector cuts that emerged from the mid-1970s, attention became more focused on defending rather than criticising public provision. By the late 1970s, the mood was switching from exposing the failures of the welfare state and demanding greater investment in public services to defending those same services that had previously been found wanting.

Community development offered an approach that stood apart from and crossed over service-specific boundaries. It was able to relate to people as citizens rather than the frequently damaged public service-related identities such as those of 'client', 'claimant' or 'tenant'. Yet this also introduced a tension within community development between those who have utilised it as a way of improving a particular public service and those initiatives focused on shaping the nature and inter-relationships of the public sphere. The former placed the practitioner in a relatively straightforward role, that of a public service professional working on service improvement. The latter was a far more ambiguous and contradictory position of working for the betterment of social democracy and public well-being. To define either the objective or the process were more fluid, uncertain and anxiety-producing tasks with greater risks for all those involved.

It was perhaps inevitable that many of those recruited to community development during this period should be sympathetic to if not partisans in the new radical social justice politics of the period and committed to a social change agenda. Indeed, there is some evidence that the Wilson government wished to recruit those with such radical leanings to the CDPs and other reform strategies. The radical left politics of community development at that time is indeed reflected in the literature and dominated its politics (Mayo, 1977; Curno, 1978). It was also felt within those organisations, mainly local government, who were the primary employers. Here community development practitioners were frequently seen to be either supporting, even encouraging or mobilising, community organisations to challenge decisions taken by both elected members and other welfare professionals, generating new demands for more or better services or social conditions, or struggling for recognition of the social rights of minority or excluded groups, and to be doing so not in a covert manner but as an explicit element of the development role. It was not surprising, therefore, that out of such conflicts, that occasionally led to workers being pressurised, disciplined or dismissed by employers too uncomfortable with the consequences of community organising, development practitioners began to critically explore the nature of their own role as well as the wider purposes of welfare provision (Cockburn, 1977; LEWRG, 1980).

Community development practitioners were not alone in this process of critical self-reflection as this was also a period of rapid growth in the membership of public service trade unions (Miller, 1996). Public sector trade union militancy grew during the latter part of the 1970s and into the 1980s as the first substantial cuts in public sector funding were introduced following the election of Margaret Thatcher with her commitment to 'rolling back the state', her crude dismissal of 'society' and elevation of the market and the legal systems as the ultimate saviours of all social problems (Loney, 1983). However, the stance of the wider trade union movement to town hall militancy was often ambivalent (Miller, 1996). Moreover, this militancy created tensions between unionised public service employees and many of those with whom they worked – clients, older people, tenants, parents, young people – who were often vulnerable and dependent on public services to meet essential needs (Puddephat, 1987). Public service trade unionists were in a double bind here – militancy to challenge cuts to services risked impacting on precisely those service users whose interests trade unionists were struggling to defend. The immediate connection between union demands for better pay and conditions and improved public services was not always sufficiently obvious (Heery, 1987; Miller, 1996). During the 1980s, as more radical local authorities with the support of the public and community organisations sought to improve services through localisation and devolution, they frequently encountered strong trade union opposition that in some instances led to the abandonment of such policies (Miller, 1996).

The divisive politics of Thatcherism were subsequently replaced by the more consensual approach of John Major, who led two Conservative governments and whose Minister of the Environment, Michael Heseltine, introduced the concept of citizen and service user 'charters' and first championed partnership working between government, communities and third sector organisations. Subsequently, the Labour Party, seeking to re-position itself in the territory of 'third way' politics, after Tony Blair's election as party leader, further developed this approach. As outlined in the previous chapter this sought to simultaneously identify a contemporary politics in which both market-driven economic growth and prosperity could go hand-in-hand with greater equality and an extension of social democracy. Further it sought to fundamentally dissociate 'new' Labour from a particular discourse described as the 'old' class-driven, divisive and 'unelectable' Labour of the 1970s and 1980s. Since the election of a Labour government in 1997, following 18 years and five neoliberal Conservative governments, disadvantaged neighbourhoods have been rebranded as 'socially excluded', disconnected from the mainstream, and as having missed out from the continuous rising living standards and improved well-being experienced by the majority.

Community organising as local agency

State-sponsored community development is not, and never has been, the only game in town. There is an alternative narrative of community organising that is part of a broader tradition of dissent. This is reflected in the collective self-activity of members of a shared community identity in pursuit of common goals or in response to some perceived external or internal threat, real or imagined. Communities of locality and communities of interest have organised, and continue to organise themselves, and to build alliances for change, working through and with civil society organisations, networks and social movements. The basis of such activity is often identical to those identified above, which triggers intervention by the state or other external agents. Indeed, local initiatives and external interventions to address the same issues often occur in parallel yet independently of each other. Increasingly, NGOs have pursued their objectives by employing their own workers. The funding for such posts is usually the outcome of successful bids for public funds that are increasingly target-driven, project-based and time-limited. This approach has resulted in increased competition between local organisations struggling to secure resources from the same limited funds, greater attention paid to organisational survival and a concomitant weakening of a shared identity both between local organisations and between the organisation and the community. It has also led to a reduction of state-employed development professionals working to a generic brief who can help maintain a common identity.

The nature of the relationship between a community and the external intervening agent, and specifically the practitioners it employs, is critical to the success of any strategy and is one that is often tense and difficult. This relationship is made more complex when the practitioner comes from a different social class to the communities s/he is working with, as the following example shows.

Rachel is a white middle-class community worker whose team has been reorganised so that she now finds herself working in an unfamiliar part of the city. Rachel's brief is specifically to work with women, and for many years she has worked in the inner-city area where she has developed considerable expertise in working with refugees and asylum seekers. However, her new patch is mainly one very large, almost entirely white and quite isolated public housing estate. There are very low levels of community activity and few community organisations that are not propped up by 'outsiders'. Rachel has begun to work with one of the few women's groups that have managed to keep going over time. The group was set up by mothers concerned by the very high levels of drug use on the estate. Rachel quickly discovers that one woman who inspires and intimidates the other members in equal measure dominates the group. Through its fundraising efforts the group has procured a minibus that is kept parked in the front garden of this domineering woman. A couple of members complain to Rachel that this woman treats the bus as if it were her own property; they add that those that are outside this woman's clique feel that they do not have the right to make suggestions about the use of the bus. Rachel also feels intimidated by this woman who in subtle ways seems able to exploit the fact that Rachel is an 'outsider' to the area. Yet she has to admit that the group has been very effective and continues to play an important role in tackling drug use on the estate even though it does not appear to be run very democratically.

While there may be exceptions, development practitioners will typically seek to make strong links with indigenous groups, organisations and activists. Where such independent and sustainable bodies do not exist the task will be to help create them. This will increase the likelihood of both a smooth introduction into the community and the chances of successfully achieving the desired outcomes. Failure to work closely with existing groups and activists is likely to create resistance and resentment that local efforts have not been recognised. Where local activists are thin on the ground development practitioners may have to build on structures that are dormant, weak or ineffective and support local activists who work on limited or narrow agendas or are overwhelmed and exhausted by the scale of the problems they face. Here the danger is that the professional practitioner may come to substitute her or himself for the absent local activists, creating a kind of pseudo-development.

Community development is committed to supporting indigenous collective action by building or strengthening autonomous community organisations and working to agendas determined by the members of the community. However, the extent to which community activity can be independent or autonomous when it has emerged entirely as a consequence of external facilitation is a matter for empirical evaluation rather than a theoretical and professional assumption. Independence comes not simply from having and controlling sufficient and secure resources over a long enough period of time but also depends on the degree to which the objectives and action plans have grown from or are owned by the community. Organisations that continue to orientate themselves primarily in relation to the state, defining themselves and their efforts in response to state [in]actions, cannot be thought of as independent. Ironically, such dependency offers a continuous supply of objects, real and imagined, against which organisations can react. In other words, if the organisational gaze is towards the state there will always be much to occupy it. However, when this becomes its primary task it becomes an unhealthy dependency.

Independence requires a capacity for reflexive thinking, to make autonomous choices to join or leave relationships, to invite others to speak to your concerns or to join with you, to pursue your chosen path. Autonomy may be an illusion, however, in a context where the state is ever more present in civil society, especially in the lives of the disadvantaged. Navigating complex and uncertain circumstances creates anxiety about the choices made and those rejected or the path chosen and the associated costs, especially in comparison to what might seem to be the relatively safe, predictable and contained relationships with another on whom one is dependent. Local community initiatives that fail to become autonomous are unlikely to be sustainable given the restricted nature of state-led interventions, the low level of resources invested, the time scales involved, the pressure of achieving targets and the shift towards contractual service-related relations.

In such circumstances local groups needing additional nourishment and support, such as capacity building, may be less likely to receive it. A cycle of local initiatives that flourish but just as quickly fade away reinforces the rationale that leads to such external intervention and may simply reproduce the cycle. Community organisations often appear trapped by a desire to be autonomous. On the one hand, there is an awareness that this is the only sustainable and ethical position to occupy and, on the other, an overriding tendency, no doubt reinforced by development workers themselves, to view the state as a progressive force committed to the advancement of social justice, greater economic equality, the protection of those at risk and the agency most able to resolve social and political conflict. Such an orientation leads community organisations to see the state as the solution to local and national concerns and leaves them lacking in financial and emotional self-sufficiency and dependent on its largesse, particularly the gift of recognition. Paradoxically, autonomous organisations may find that others do not always welcome this independence including those agencies involved in their initial development. Independent voices may be the stated outcome of any community development intervention but can be too uncomfortable in practice.

The relationship between the professional practitioner and local communities can be further complicated when the practitioner has been recruited from the local community itself. Activists who become paid practitioners are likely to experience conflicting loyalties and considerable role strain as the following example illustrates.

Carol works for a community partnership on the public housing estate where she grew up and still lives to this day. She got into paid work through her long involvement in local schools that she felt had very low expectations of local children. After years of work on Parent Teacher Associations and as a school governor for several local schools Carol was invited to join the local community partnership, which had recently received over £20 million funding under the government's Single Regeneration Budget. They were looking for someone to spearhead their education work and Carol was the natural person for the job. Part of Carol's job is to operate a community budget for funding local groups and projects. Decisions are made by a steering group of local residents who are members of the partnership board. Carol's role is to advise the steering group. Local groups perceive Carol as having the key influence over a popular budget for which there is fierce competition. Before taking up her post Carol had been a long-standing member of one of these groups, one that puts on play schemes throughout the summer holidays. Carol was desperate to avoid accusations of favouritism but, following decisions made by the steering group which forced a scaling back of play schemes on the local estate that year, she now found herself accused of betrayal by her 'own' group and faced by rumours to the effect that 'now she had got her job she was turning her back on her friends and allies'.

Many local policy makers, funding bodies and managers have come to believe the most effective interventions are likely to be carried out by practitioners who are able to empathise with the target communities and communicate in ways that resonate with those populations. As a consequence there has been a commitment to recruiting those who are from disadvantaged communities but this can pose some awkward issues in itself. Many recruited in this way receive little formal training, particularly of a theoretical nature. Yet without a theoretical grasp of the nature of the state, of structural inequality, of the history of development work and the various uses to which it has been put there is a danger that when local activists become professionalised they miss out on some of the equipment that might help them sustain a critical approach to their work. Moreover, increased social diversity has led to a greater cultural relativism and this in turn can encourage a 'live and let live' approach, which can enable bad practice to go unchallenged, all under the guise of cultural sensitivity.

Capacities required of the capacity builders

Some uncertainty continues to surround the requirements and expectations of development practitioners (Mayo et al, 2007c). Such ambiguity is in part related to the belief that sustainable development comes from within. Consequently there is a desire to recognise and improve, through informal and increasingly formal training, the skills and capacities of community activists, who may be paid or unpaid but are not professionally qualified. As we have just seen, those activists who choose to pursue a career in community development by gaining a professional qualification and competing in the labour market face repeated questioning of themselves and by others as to their identity, loyalty and motivation. Support and recognition for citizen activists sits sometimes uncomfortably with the view that, as a strategic state intervention, development work should be carried out by qualified professionals in much the same way as other welfare professionals. Yet experience also suggests that those practitioners who are able to empathise with the target communities and communicate in ways that resonate with those populations implement effective interventions. Such skills are not always present in professional training nor are they necessarily part of the personal repertoire of those who might be attracted to a public service career. As a result, training providers and employers have been inclined to seek out those who are themselves from the 'communities', broadly defined, that are likely to be the objects of intervention as well as those who are able to identify with such communities and are committed to the values of development. Such recruitment policies create a tension within the workforce when professionals have personal political commitments that conflict with those of the employer, despite the apparent congruity between them. In other words, development practitioners can frequently experience themselves as being both 'in and against the state'.

The negotiation of such conflicts of interest has been made more complex by two factors. The first is that community development is often located on the margins of the organisation, in relation to other welfare professionals. This is especially the case in state organisations where development professionals are both small in number and employed in departments dominated by other professions unfamiliar with the objectives and methods of development and sometimes hostile to its outcomes, especially when the outcomes imply a critique of their own practice. Secondly, development professionals are often physically located away from the main organisational base and working on their own or with few others. Too often they are managed by those who themselves have no direct experience or understanding of the practice and philosophy of development and are unable to provide the necessary support. Occasionally, when development is team-based and more strategically located, as in the office of the chief executive or corporate development, and able to have a direct influence on policy, it can be a source of resentment for other professionals who have less access to decision-making processes or elected members. When located close to the 'centre of power' in this way practitioners may be seduced into speaking on behalf of communities, as a self-appointed community 'voice', a voice which is more easily managed than the real thing. This can be a tempting option to take when communities are locked out of decision making.

Community participation and development strategies in the global South: comparisons and contrasts

The current UK government's propensity for a community-related approach is not the only case in point. Other national and local governments and international bodies including supra-national governmental organisations have adopted community development strategies for a variety of motives. In the context of neoliberal processes of globalisation, there has also been increasing interest in identifying comparisons and contrasts with experiences elsewhere, sharing learning across national and international boundaries, especially from experiences in the global South. Such mutual learning also acknowledges the limitations of previous assumptions about learning as a one-way process, assumptions all too often rooted in the colonial past. The histories of colonial and other Western programmes to promote community development were far from representing the whole story. On the contrary, as Rajesh Tandon and others have pointed out, the history of people-led struggles for participatory approaches to development dates back to the end of the Second World War, and the actions of movements for colonial freedom (Tandon, 2008). It was, of course, the case that top-down expert-led approaches were being promoted at this time. In India, for example, the Ford Foundation and USAID supported the community development programme from the early 1950s. By the late 1960s, and the early 1970s, however, alternative approaches began to emerge on the development agenda.

In the words of one of the key proponents, 'The 1970s saw a sudden increase in writings related to bottom-up, people-led participatory development' (Tandon, 2008). The work of Paulo Freire in Brazil and elsewhere was seminal. In addition, Tandon also identified the influence of Gandhian philosophy, 'putting people at the centre', which was the thrust of Julius Nyerere's approach in Tanzania, for example. Participatory approaches, including participatory approaches to action research, spread across the global South as well as impacting on the development of theory and practice in the global North. Community development and community education has been profoundly influenced by these approaches, Freire's contribution being recognised as underpinning government programmes in Britain whether or not these approaches have been distorted in the process of being imported.

By the late 1980s, participation had been effectively mainstreamed in large-scale development programmes. This was, in part at least, due to international agencies' and national governments' concerns to mitigate the negative effects of the rampant neoliberalism of the early 1980s, countering social fragmentation, increasing polarisation and poverty through the active participation of the poor themselves (Mayo and Craig, 1995). The poor were to be encouraged to stand on their own two feet (pull themselves up by their bootstraps if they had any) while further bypassing and thereby further marginalising the public provision of services to meet increasing needs. Participation has been termed the 'new tyranny' (Cooke and Kothari, 2001) – one more hoop for the poor to jump through in their struggles for survival, let alone development.

As Cornwall, among others, has pointed out, like community development, 'Participation has a long and chequered history' (Cornwall, 2008). The point to emphasise here is simply this. Like community development, participation can be promoted from the top down in ways that are potentially controlling and even divisive. Or alternatively, participation can contribute to more transformative agendas. 'The challenge for community development', it has been suggested, 'is to be able to both enable those who take up these seats (in invited spaces for participation) to exercise voice and influence, and to help provide whatever support is needed – material, moral and political – to popular mobilisation that seeks to influence policy through advocacy rather than negotiation' (Cornwall, 2008). The state, Cornwall concludes:

> … has a role to play in this, especially in respect of marginalised groups (Young, 2000), and taking up that role accountably and supportively – without taking "over", and tutoring "the people" to speak to power in "acceptable" ways (Barnes, 2006) – is one of the challenges that efforts to stimulate community development through participation needs to address. (Cornwall, 2008)

This conclusion would seem to be equally relevant for the global North as well as for the global South.

Current context

Today the language of community dominates the policy landscape of both northern and southern nation states in a way that seems unprecedented. International policy transfer is increasingly commonplace as is the adoption of explanatory concepts and resultant practices, often with insufficient regard for local contexts. Thus the language of 'social exclusion', 'stronger sustainable communities', 'local governance', 'capacity building', 'citizen choice', 'social capital', 'empowerment' and 'democratic deficit' is as familiar in Australia and Nicaragua as it is in the US, Bulgaria, Southern Africa and Britain.

Reflecting on community development in the current context in Britain, Mae Shaw has summarised its history and contemporary challenges, pointing to its ambivalent relationship with the state and with democracy. 'As a profession it was created as a means of managing or mediating the relationship between the state and its population' she argued, 'particularly in circumstances of crisis here and abroad' (Shaw, 2008b, p 13). Community development, she continued, 'embodies a central tension between the demands of policy and the demands of democratic politics which are not always or automatically compatible. Framed around an egalitarian democratic discourse, it has been deployed by successive governments of different ideological persuasions to pre-empt trouble and to deliver policy objectives as much as to challenge power and engage with communities in any serious way' (Shaw, 2008b, p 13).

In the current context, Shaw went on to argue, there was, in her view, 'a crisis at the heart of all democratic projects, particularly those enacted and funded by the state, such as community development. This crisis', she continued, 'stems directly from neo-liberal economics and the Third Way politics that attempts to manage it. Social and democratic purposes may continue to dominate professional discourses of practice, but economic objectives are increasingly applied to community development as policy. This is translated in community contexts', she concluded 'through various kinds of service delivery and managed governance as gate-keeping rather than enabling, with profound implications for community development' (Shaw, 2008b, p 14). While the balance may have shifted, we suggest that these contradictory directional pulls have always been present and that the relationships between them are different according to local and policy contexts. Similarly, the extent to which any activity can be understood as 'gate-keeping' or 'enabling' is itself a dilemma long familiar in community development and would only have profound implications if 'managed governance' was felt to be incompatible with development or inappropriate. Not for the first time, 'Community development has been centrally implicated in the transformation of the welfare landscape as a key agent of the "modernisation" agenda: facilitating partnership working, enacting standardised standards of community engagement, involved in capacity building around pre-determined outcomes, managing the audit and measurement culture, brokering the contract culture, remoralising communities through deficit models of engagement' (Shaw, 2008b, p 15). What is strikingly different in this period is that in this relatively unfamiliar role as a key transformative agent the contradictions inherent to development work, and indeed those of 'new' Labour, and the consequent dilemmas and challenges are sharply exposed.

There are, however, some tensions here, as communities are being invited to devise their own solutions, with increasing emphasis on decentralisation, right down to the local level. Yet governments may be simultaneously pointing to the limitations of effective action even at the national level, let alone at these more local levels. Third way politics defines itself through a discourse of global uncertainty and calls for a shift in expectations about what the state can provide (Powell, 2000). Neoliberal agendas predominate, in other words. The logic of such a position, characteristic of Third Way-type approaches such as those adopted by successive New Labour governments, has been to restrict state interventions, focusing on mitigating the social costs, rather than challenging the underlying causes. Such an approach would seem to be reducing the scope for community action at the local level.

Meanwhile neoliberalism has reinforced the notion of the citizen as an autonomous individual, an independent but rational and responsible subject, pursuing his or her own self-defined interests. This is, of course, despite the fact that individuals are also social beings, individuals whose choices are also shaped by a range of influences and factors, subconscious and irrational as well as rationally self-interested, motivated by collective as well as individualistic concerns. There are fundamental tensions, then, for community development work, in the contemporary context, shaped so significantly, as it has been, by neoliberal agendas and processes of globalisation.

As subsequent chapters argue, the current policy focus on 'community' does offer new spaces and opportunities for community action, both locally and beyond, linking local citizen actions with broader coalitions, internationally. But these opportunities and spaces are also inherently problematic and challenging. Working within such a policy framework confronts development practitioners with a series of contemporary dilemmas. For those inspired by the potential contribution that development work could make, working towards an alternative vision of equity and social justice, these dilemmas are to be felt most sharply.

FOUR

The resilience of development workers

Development work as a growing occupation

We traced the history of development work in Chapter Three and in doing so noted the changing nature of this work in Britain and the developing world. As development work has become seen as the answer to a growing number of problems (of governance, economic development and social justice), so more and more practitioners have been drawn under its umbrella.

The number of front-line staff being paid to engage in work with British communities has increased significantly in recent years. Since 1997 a trickle of programmes to involve communities and service users has turned into a veritable flood of initiatives to promote participation, capacity building and partnership working. Precise job numbers are difficult to obtain, as this type of employment is something of a moving target in the current context, characterised by the increasing use of short-term contracts to work in time-limited projects. One recent UK-government supported survey carried out between 2001 and 2003 by the Community Development Foundation (CDF) and the Standing Conference on Community Development (SCCD) estimated that some 14,000 were employed by the beginning of the 21st century, compared with some 5,000 such staff in the 1980s (Glen et al, 2004). In contrast, the National Training Organisation *PAULO* put its estimate as high as 146,000. The majority of posts in the CDF/SCCD survey were dependent on central or local government funding, either directly or indirectly via special initiatives, although over half the staff were employed in the voluntary sector.

While welcoming this expansion of official support, the survey raised a number of concerns about the quality of jobs being created. Only just over half of the staff had permanent contracts, with some indication that there had been a decline in the proportion of permanent posts. The pay was modest and women were disproportionately likely to be among the lower paid in what was becoming an increasingly feminised workforce (around two thirds of the workforce was female compared with just over half in the mid-1980s). This casualisation – and the associated deterioration in professional conditions – was a cause for some concern. As a participant commented in one of the subsequent workshops, "initiatives come and go so quickly [it] undermines community confidence and community development is harder than ten years ago". Not only do community groups become tired of the constant turnover of staff (Glen et al, 2004, p 18) but there are stresses inherent in trying to combine professional values with the requirements of a 'contract culture'. Not surprisingly perhaps, workers highlighted the need for more strategic approaches and more emphasis on professional values (Glen et al, 2004). The job of paid workers was experienced as having become more complex, involving a wider range of issues, from regeneration and local economic development to community safety and crime reduction, from anti-poverty strategies and social inclusion to health, housing and planning and regeneration via community arts. Three quarters were involved in capacity building and two thirds were involved in facilitating or supporting self-help and/or consultation (compared with just over a third who were involved in advocacy and over a third who spent less than 25% of their time working directly with communities).

Development workers in the research

The development practitioners in the research came from diverse social and personal backgrounds. Some of them were community development workers, but others came from related professions, including youth work, education (including adult community education), health promotion, community safety and urban regeneration. Despite the variety of contexts, however, they all worked with communities as a major part of their professional role, or as a major factor in their lives, as professionals who had become so involved in surrounding communities that they had taken on key roles as community representatives on structures of governance. They included those from professional middle-class homes as well as those from working-class backgrounds, from families with strong public service values and conversely from families where this was not particularly marked. In some cases, early experiences had been problematic in the extreme – including domestic violence, family breakdown and experiences of life in care, including experiences of abuse. Others had experienced loss through migration, including that of becoming a refugee.

The great majority of participants had ended up in development work rather than it being the outcome of a conscious career. Yet if happenstance was the dominant explanation, their current occupations were by no means random professional outcomes. Rather, as we will see in the next chapter, it seemed to be more of an expression of who they were, a part of their identity. Most lacked a shared professional framework but came from other older professional formations such as youth work, community development, health promotion, housing management, social work and education. While the majority were untrained, those who were trained had qualified in community development work, which exemplifies an aspect of work performed by other human services professionals.

Ethical and emotional demands of development work

Development work is concerned to promote a particular kind of learning and change, one that is sometimes referred to as 'learning to learn' or 'second order' change (Bateson, 1972). It is the difference between acquiring learning and acquiring *the capacity* to learn, or 'sustainable' learning. Second order change is concerned with longer-term sustainable internal transformations within the individual or group through relationship building and emotional engagement. It is concerned to facilitate the development of those human capacities – intellectual, practical, emotional and moral, among others – necessary for contemporary citizenship. The uniqueness of social development work is that its focus is primarily the group rather than the individual. Development goals are not easily measurable and they find expression in outcomes rather than outputs. Such changes often occur in non-linear ways as a result of thoughtful and systemically oriented interventions, which do not sit comfortably within the currently dominant rationalising strategy (Miller et al, 2006).

The following example, from an interview with Si, a youth worker with over 20 years' experience, provides a vivid example of the issues at stake here.

'There's a young girl come into the youth centre and she looks very miserable, she's just an appendage of her boyfriend, and she takes no part in anything that's going on. She's just around. Takes a while to find out who she is. But she keeps coming. Now unlike other professionals, we've got no assessment plan for her, we've got no initial interview, we've got no needs assessment; she's just coming. And then at some point and I don't know why, but she chose to talk to one of the members of staff here about a range of things, quite big things, family relationships, living arrangements, lack of schooling, and an eating disorder. Quite big stuff. Now [the worker] was able to respond to that, managed to talk to housing people about housing, 'cos it seemed that that was the only one that could possibly be solved…. Now she isn't actually moving out, getting a flat, but the striking thing about her is she started smiling when she came into the youth centre, which felt like a real achievement. And she started, she started looking comfortable, and she started looking healthier and she started to involve herself in stuff that was going on, right. And talking with people, and really articulating, and being keen about things and organising things. Now when she came in, we had no idea what it was that would end. But it's a question of being, of being patient, knowing that sometimes something will happen. And she's around, and she will take her time and all we've got to do is wait, but we've got to be damn well ready for it when it happens … so a lot of the work at the moment, we're asked to give targets to what we will achieve. Well that one, I wouldn't have been able to target. And even now, the outcome – like she smiled…. Through her contact with us she has managed to resolve things within herself, and we've been part of that process.'

This is a telling example of good practice that illustrates the capacity of an institution and its staff to be receptive and the value of just 'being with' rather than 'doing', or, as Margot Waddell (1989) once put it, the value of service as opposed to servicing. The institution does not present itself as an agency that is trying to do something to the girl but as one that makes itself available to be used by her, the crucial change she resolves within herself. This example also tells us something crucial about development work that, we would add, is a component of all human service relationships.

Development rarely occurs as a result of the simple linear processes of causation that are implied by input–output models of performance management. In the example above, development occurred as a consequence of noticing, waiting, being patient, not intervening prematurely and then responding effectively at the right moment. Development is not 'caused' but emerges, effective intervention is not so much about 'acting on' but 'providing the necessary conditions'. In complex systems things cannot be predicted or controlled – why did the girl choose to approach that member of staff, at that moment?

Emotional challenges: social suffering

The following example comes from Si again. He is referring to a recent incident in which some youths trashed his club and then three of them – two brothers and their friend's cousin – turned on each other. The younger brother is known to be dangerous and has used knives in the past.

'The younger brother and the other protagonist were just yelling abuse at each other. And they just sounded so hysterical, fragile and upset. I mean that was quite upsetting, because they were both saying really hurtful things to each other. I mean when I find this, all of them have actually got quite a lot of pain in their backgrounds and they scratch at each other's pain, they don't let it, they don't show solidarity for other people. On these situations they actually pull at the scabs you know, yelling awful things about their parents, the majority of which were true, you know.'

Poverty and exclusion generate 'social suffering' (Bourdieu, 1999), the 'hidden injuries' of class, 'race' and other oppressions, and development professionals work with the resulting anger and despair on a daily basis. One of the effects of combining neoliberalism and globalisation is to vastly increase social inequalities so that poverty grows in both the absolute and relative sense while routes out of poverty, despite government rhetoric, become increasingly restricted. Poverty and marginalisation assume starkly spatial forms. This is particularly evident in the US and some newly industrialising countries such as India, where affluent gated communities and ghettos exist in proximate but parallel worlds. But the same phenomenon, in milder form, can be perceived in Britain, France and many other democracies where large and often isolated public housing estates become populated by large concentrations of the poor working class. In a country like Britain, where rates of social mobility are very low, parallel processes of education segregation and geographical isolation from the main labour markets reproduce the spatial segregation of poor working-class communities. The structural lock-in that befalls such communities is masked by social policies that then blame such groups for their own lack of education and economic progress. They become subject to new forms of pathologisation – now located in dysfunctional family systems and social networks rather than, as in the 1950s and 1960s, in individuals themselves. All of these processes combine to produce a 'pressure cooker' effect on poor communities, and if the growing tension cannot find an external outlet in struggles for social justice, then the pressures become 'internalised' within these communities, leading to growing despair, self-harming behaviour such as drug abuse and the projection of hurts and frustrations onto friends, families and neighbours (picking at the scabs), often in the form of racist, sexist or homophobic abuse. Scarce communal resources can also be fought over by different factions, often in underhand ways. Several workers in our sample had faced issues of corruption in community organisations that they had to deal with.

It follows that development workers find themselves working on a daily basis with troubled individuals and groups and having to deal with interpersonal conflicts, group rivalries and sometimes oppressive behaviours that are meted out across the divisions of class, gender or 'race'. Development workers in this situation may themselves easily become the target of abuse:

> 'I really think about the shit that, you know when you go and do community development on estates and you go to meeting after meeting and you get abused and people tell you you're stealing their resources and all kinds of things. They accuse you of heinous things and treat you like a piece of shit and you have nowhere to go with that except for home and like, you know, to whatever, at the bottom of whatever bottle or spliff or whatever.'

These are the words of a female community worker in London with over 15 years' experience in the field. They are fairly typical of the experiences of some of our sample, particularly the experience of having nowhere "to take the shit" but home. This woman has now left this kind of work and has gone to work for a voluntary organisation focusing on self-harming behaviour in teenagers. The nature of development work, then, is such that the emotional demands that it makes on workers are extremely high.

Ethical challenges

In previous chapters we examined some of the structural and institutional factors that place development workers in tricky, ambiguous and contested positions. We considered three dimensions of this:

- Development workers operate on the boundary between state and civil society.
- The different communities that make up local civil society typically have different values, and tensions often exist between generations, sexes and different faiths and cultures.
- Government policies towards these communities are constantly changing, often inconsistent or even contradictory.

These three dimensions are briefly highlighted here.

State and civil society: the agendas of government employers or state/ NGO funders will often conflict with the needs of local communities. Development workers will find themselves in the middle of these conflicting requirements. Available funding may be for social capacity building whereas what may be most required is rebuilding the physical infrastructure, or, more usually these days, funding is short term, designed to make a big splash, whereas what is needed is a longer-term commitment. Often development workers will have a brief to enable local communities to set their own agendas but they will sometimes find that if they pursue this brief too vigorously they will be blamed by employers for stirring up conflict. Torn by conflicting loyalties, haunted by the question 'whose side are you on?', development workers often find themselves in a 'no win' situation.

Contested communities: the development worker's brief is made more complex because local civil society is itself very heterogeneous. There is no such thing as 'community' if this is thought of as some undifferentiated unity; even apparently homogeneous 'faith communities' will contain generational and gendered differences. Identifying community needs is therefore a complex task that, if it fails to include all relevant stakeholders, will inevitably lead to the privileging of some agendas over others. Development workers can easily get caught up in these differences and may, for example, run the risk of being seen as disloyal by older people if they give too much priority to the voices and needs of disaffected young people.

Inconsistent policies: we consider these in more detail in Chapter Nine. Suffice to say here, as Michael Lipsky (1980) noted long ago, one of the means by which governments 'resolve' apparently irresolvable policy conflicts is by passing the intractable contradictions down the line to front-line staff.

Development workers deal with multiple, complex and often competing agendas and must exercise agency within a loose and shifting framework. They are required to balance the competing demands of immediate service users, commitments to a vision of a wider society as well as employer and government policy. Yet, as we saw in Chapter One, development work is occurring in a context in which ethical conduct is far from obvious (Bauman, 1993), where the ethical subject must function within 'dilemmatic spaces' in which choices are ambiguous, indeterminate and contested (Honig, 1996).

Development workers therefore need to have the capacity to make fine ethical judgements and, as we saw in Chapter One, be able to risk 'acting for the best' where there is no obvious right thing to do. Development workers need to be able to cope with criticism from all sides, from both funding bodies and employers and from local activists, and yet sustain a sense of self-worth and morale without which their motivation can easily crumble.

When caught in a dilemma, an individual typically experiences anxiety because of the uncertainty regarding what is the right thing to do. Then, when choosing one course of action and rejecting another, guilt and regret may be felt towards the rejected alternative (Williams, 1973, 1981). Interestingly, our research suggested that the intensity of the emotions involved – anxiety, unhappiness, doubt, guilt – was no less great where professionals had little or no choice regarding the decision being made. However, while for most the dilemmas of the job are a source of stress, for some they can be a source of satisfaction. As one person expressed it,

> 'I think the fact that there are those things, dilemmas, conflicts and tensions … makes the job interesting. Certainly it's the same with a lotta jobs … if you've got a crisis … you kinda want the crisis, need the crisis situation to make yourself more effective. There's a bit of that in this job, it's a terrible thing to say but if organisations go pear shaped, it's quite interesting, it's an interesting bit of the job. If … it's all running well, it's not that interesting to be honest.'

Coping with stress: the theory

To summarise, development work poses many ethical and emotional challenges and yet, as we shall see later, many workers operate in quite isolated circumstances with little professional or managerial support. Unsurprisingly this work can be highly stressful and the uncertain nature of the employment contracts of many of these workers contributes to high rates of labour turnover. What enables some workers to operate in such conditions more effectively than others? This is an important question, with implications for training and management as well as for the way in which the workers manage themselves.

We know very little about burnout in political activists (Downton and Wehr, 1997; Wakefield and Purdue, 2007), and while there is an enormous volume of research focusing on stress and burnout at work, only a very small part of this specifically focuses on human services work (Briner et al, 2007). In their overview of the general literature, Rob Briner and his colleagues note that burnout classically has three primary symptoms: emotional exhaustion, cynicism and low accomplishment. General precipitating factors include size of the workload, the extent of the worker's autonomy and control over aspects of the job, role conflict and role ambiguity. Briner et al suggest that one of the distinctive aspects of human services work lies in the emotional demands of the job, but one of the few pieces of previous research specifically on human services workers found no correlation between the emotionally demanding nature of the work and levels of burnout. Briner et al suggest the key mitigating factor here appears to lie in the commitment of these workers to their work, in other words, their high levels of commitment somehow enable them to deal with the emotional demands of the job more effectively.

There is another body of research that is relevant. Over the past 30 years a body of research has developed, sometimes referred to as the 'stress and coping paradigm', which has examined the differential capacity of adults living in poverty to cope with the stresses of their lives. This approach provides a useful framework with which to understand those factors that also enables development workers to cope effectively with the ethical and emotional demands of their jobs. Essentially this approach suggests that the amount of stress a person experiences will vary according to the internal and external resources that they have and the coping styles and strategies that they adopt (Pearlin et al, 1981; Garmezy and Rutter, 1983; Brown et al, 1986).

Personal and social resources

External or social resources include the strength of a person's intimate ties, particularly the presence of close friends or family members in whom they can confide, and social networks. Supportive social networks can include neighbours, colleagues, members of faith groups, clubs, and so on. The value of such resources in enabling all workers to handle stress is also well documented in the stress at work literature (Briner et al, 2007). External resources can also include the availability of more 'material' forms of support such as access to activities contributing to 'pressure release', the use of food, drink, opiates and other forms of 'comfort' and so on.

Internal or personal resources have been less well researched (Turner and Lloyd, 1999) but appear to include the 'steeling effect' which contributes to the feeling of invulnerability in stressful situations (Garmezy, 1983), positive self-regard and the belief in one's own capacity to be able to shape the course of events, referred to as 'internal locus of control' (Mirowsky and Ross, 1990), and indeed the importance of having a 'sense of mattering' (Taylor and Turner, 2001).

The model argues that individuals respond in different ways to similar potential sources of stress as a result of the personal and social resources that they have available. Because of these resources, individuals perceive potentially stressful events in different ways, as we saw at the end of the previous section. Lazarus and Folkman (1984) refer to this as 'cognitive appraisal' – the different meanings that different individuals give to similar events in their lives.

Coping styles and strategies

Lazarus and Folkman (1984) draw attention to the importance of an individual's 'coping styles'. They imply that there are a variety of coping styles that an individual may make use of, such as 'avoidant coping, characterized by knowing little and not wanting to know, to the other extreme of vigilant coping in which they had much information and welcomed still more' (1984, p 129), but that particular individuals may also have preferred styles. After a survey of the literature they emphasise that the attempt to cope by asserting agency or mastery, which much of the literature implies is the most effective response, may reflect 'deeply ingrained Western values' that 'venerate mastery over the environment as the coping ideal' (1984, p 138). They continue:

> The problem here is not that solving problems is undesirable, but not all sources of stress in living are amenable to mastery, or even fit within a problem-solving framework.... Emphasising problem solving and mastery devalues other functions of coping that are concerned with *managing emotions* and maintaining self-esteem and positive outlook, especially in the face of irremediable situations. Coping processes that are used to tolerate such difficulties, or to minimize, accept or ignore them, are just as important ... as problem solving strategies that aim to master the environment. (Lazarus and Folkman, 1984, pp 138-9; emphasis added)

By challenging the 'Western' valuation of coping as mastery over the environment Lazarus and Folkman are able to make a crucial distinction between what they call *problem-focused coping* and *emotion-focused coping* (1984, pp 151–5). They define coping thus: '… as constantly changing cognitive and behavioural efforts to manage specific external and/or internal demands that are appraised as taxing or exceeding the resources of the person' (p 14). Note here the emphasis on 'managing' rather than 'overcoming' or 'resolving'; note also the emphasis on internal as well as external demands. The (internal) demands of conscience, manifest in the guilty feeling that one is not doing enough, can be a powerful source of stress. Wakefield and Purdue (2007), for example, found guilt to be a major source of stress for environmental activists. Similarly, when your work brings you face to face with poverty and social suffering, there may seem to be no limits to the needs that the development worker should address.

Coping with stress: the practice

External resources: supervision and management support

The national UK survey conducted by CDF/SCCD expressed serious concerns about the level of training and support available to development workers, the paucity of which led to 'a substantial risk in some situations for alienation and burn out in those most likely to operate in facilitation roles' (Gaffney, 2002, p 20). Supervision was all too often found to be inadequate, 'there is no time to receive supervision', commented one worker 'as we're delivering targets' (quoted in Glen et al, 2004, p 37). And even when supervision was forthcoming, this was not necessarily being delivered by colleagues with the relevant expertise. A quarter of the respondents in the CDF/SCCD survey were being supervised by someone with no direct experience of working with communities and 40% were being supervised by someone not currently practising community development work. As one of the respondents commented, 'workers can be left in the middle without strategic thinking or direction' (quoted in Glen et al, 2004, p 38).

Many of the workers in our sample found that management unwittingly undermined them through the very way they made support available. As one worker put it,

> 'Well, the work is very emotional. Now when I've said this the manager has said, "Well, as a manager what can I do?" … he thought he was being very friendly, like what support mechanisms can I put in place, blah, blah, blah. All I wanted him to say is "It must be difficult". Right? That's all you

needed; you just need recognition of it.... And what you don't want is to have to ask for help. Because that's a kind of, it's almost like a pleading, as if the job's too difficult. So quite often youth workers don't go and ask for it, because you're then treated as if you're failing.'

These comments were echoed by a younger youth worker, Steve, who was trying to explain to the interviewer why he had paid for his own professional supervision for several years:

'I've always been very wary about showing vulnerability within this job. So even if things had been really hard, you know, and I've wanted to go home and I've wanted to cry and, you know, it was that bad, you know, I've been very reluctant to tell my managers that you know. Because, you know, that's ... you know, weakness doesn't go very far within corporate life.'

Another participant put it thus:

'There is a kind of feeling that if you bring things up like that, it's a bit dangerous because it feels like an admission of weakness that is then held against you. People would be looking at personnel policies like, do you need some time off or those sort of thing, but they're all very instrumental and structural, there isn't just that, "are you ok, that's difficult but I appreciate you're doing it", or anything like that.'

This lack of support seems to run across the statutory and voluntary/ community sectors, although there may be additional problems for those working in small voluntary or community sector organisations and agencies where specialist centralised advice is unlikely to be available and individual workers have little option but to act alone. A very small minority did refer to the excellent support that they enjoyed from their line managers. While such examples were the exception, the potential value of good formal supervision was very much recognised. Indeed, there were a few examples of workers paying privately for non-managerial supervision because they recognised its value, but had been unable to obtain this in their work settings, as Steve had.

In some cases, professionals were not just feeling unsupported by the formal structures; there were examples of instances where they had felt positively undermined by lack of management support. In one example, management simply shied away from dealing with a staffing issue, leaving the professional who had raised this out on a limb, totally unsupported, on their own.

External resources: putting your own support together

Front-line professionals too often find themselves effectively tasked with developing their own support structures, if they are to cope, personally, without burnout, in the longer term. Most were coping as best they could, by themselves, typically constructing their own personal support systems through informal networks of current and former colleagues, both within their own organisation or elsewhere, and trusted friends. Some reported regularly emailing former colleagues to share dilemmas, for example, or testing out potential solutions informally with trusted colleagues in neighbouring areas. And more personal coping strategies were also often identified – well-tried and tested ways of managing stress such as going to a football match, playing computer games, going for a drink with friends, ways of turning off at the end of a particularly stressful day (Mayo et al, 2007c). Somehow development professionals *are* finding their own ways of coping, but typically they are doing this on their own, without professional support.

All participants, regardless of length of experience, expressed strong views about the importance of space for reflection and the absence of such opportunities in their normal working lives. Consequently, although the research interview process was time consuming and even challenging, the participants who lead very busy professional lives expressed appreciation of the time and space for reflection.

Internal resources

We were struck by the enormous resilience displayed by the majority of workers in our sample, some of whom, for example, chose to work with a single community for over 20 years. This has echoes in research on social movement activists. Downton and Wehr (1997) gave the term 'persisters' to the subgroup in their own sample of peace activists who sustained a consistent level of commitment over a long period of time rather than oscillating between over-commitment and burnout. While many of the workers in our research did adopt conscious coping strategies, their resilience often appeared to be the legacy of their life history. As one of our respondents put it, "I think it probably comes from having to be a survivor". For example, in our sample of 30 workers, two had been brought up in care homes, three had experienced rape or sexual abuse, two had grown up in families marked by domestic violence, and five had experienced the deaths of significant others (mostly fathers) in early childhood. As we have seen, existing analyses of 'resilience' such as the 'stress process' model focus on the way in which experience of stressful life events can be mediated by the internal and external resources available to agents. Our research suggests that the capacity to survive difficult life experiences can itself be a source of resilience.

The research has thrown considerable light on some of the other personal resources that workers bring to the development task. We like to think of these resources as 'the capacities of the capacity builders'. Besides resilience, which we might think of as the capacity to endure, two other capacities have emerged as crucial. First, there is the capacity to stay with complexity, something we explore in more detail in the following chapter. This appears to include the capacity to contain emotional complexity, to take the standpoint of the other while not losing one's own position, to face what is often a difficult and painful reality without illusion, to be both self-aware and aware of the class, 'race' and gender dynamics of the relations in which one is immersed, and to avoid resorting to the kinds of destructive splitting which creates simplified good/bad, us/them, dichotomies. We see this capacity to contain complexity as one which contributes to 'reflexive practice', a concept that is much spoken of in the professions but little understood. Taylor and White's (2000) volume, drawing strongly on discourse psychology, is a welcome exception and we hope our research will add a psycho-social perspective that gives a stronger emphasis to the affective dimension. The second important capacity, one we explore in more detail in Chapter Seven, concerns the agent's capacity for self-authorisation – their capacity to take a stand, to operate in shifting and ambiguous situations without becoming paralysed by the uncertainty, and to act and make decisions *and* to accept the risks accompanying this (including the risk that good decisions may have bad consequences).

Coping: tricks of the trade

In one of our group discussions with participants a rich account of coping strategies and resources emerged. The pressures arising from constant change were discussed and the issue of whether or not professionals were finding that they needed to 'travel light' – not to carry too many attachments – if they were to cope with continuing organisational turbulence. On the contrary, one said, "I couldn't have survived without some of that baggage"; participants agreed.

Networking and contacts were central to the job, key in building alliances and support for partnership working, for example. Networking also emerged as centrally important to personal coping strategies – having one or more groups of colleagues and/or trusted friends with whom it would be possible to offload or "vent off", as one participant expressed it, trying out ideas and possible solutions together.

On coping more generally, in personal terms, participants spoke of the importance of listening and reflecting and being able to "hold on to being myself" – to "remember how you coped when you were feeling good", one participant added. Clarify your own role and responsibilities, she suggested, and also let go when you are not in a position to make things happen. Knowing "when to cut out", was seen as important – recognising "when it's not going to shift and it's time to split" reflected another. Similarly, even when emotionally upset (after being verbally abused at a meeting), it was important to rationalise this, it was argued, to understand why this was happening rather than taking it too personally. Boundaries were seen as key to coping.

Related to this, a number of participants commented on the importance of addressing issues and conflicts openly and honestly too, as, "It won't go away if you ignore it". Examples of conflicts that needed to be addressed included the problems caused by under-performing colleagues in general and the very specific difficulties associated with the need to challenge racism and not to shy away from issues for fear that someone might play the 'racism' card.

There were also a number of very practical suggestions about ways of exercising authority effectively. It was vitally important to keep close records including notes of meetings, especially when dealing with difficult human relations issues or dealing with conflicts with colleagues and/or managers, for example. Detailed notes (including emails) may be required for tribunals, for instance. Another participant reflected on the fine line that he tried to keep between listening to community representatives respectfully and also moving things on. Sometimes it was helpful to work with a colleague using a 'good cop and bad cop' tactic. This particular individual referred to himself as sometimes being Jekyll and sometimes Hyde in this regard. It was important, however, not to allow yourself to be pigeonholed into a particular role.

Humour emerged as a weapon as well as a defensive tactic from a number of the interviews. Several participants also emphasised the importance of remembering not to panic and the importance if needed of giving people time to respond. Losing your temper was to be avoided although there were occasions when demonstrating anger could be positive and help to move things on – another example of the use of emotions as part of coping strategies in development work.

Coping strategies: managing the person in the role

Whether consciously or unconsciously, we never simply passively accept roles, we shape them according to who we are, that is, according to our values and identity. In this way we personalise our role, bring our own personal style and characteristics to it. Sometimes this means it is not easy to separate ourselves from the roles we play. For example, Kath had been brought up in a family that contained a violent, drunk father where she often found herself protecting her mother and brothers from her father's rages. As a development worker she often found herself being called on by colleagues to mediate in conflictual situations, something she felt very ambivalent about. It was only as she talked to us in an interview situation that she began to realise where her valency for this kind of role had come from.

Deacon and Mann (1999, p 427), commenting on the normative foundation of welfare, suggest that 'the moral voice can come from within – the inner or personal voice – or from without – the external or communal voice'. We suggest that it is actually always both. In ways we do not yet fully understand, our values are always both personal and political, the outcome of some kind of dialectical interplay between the internalisations and identifications which arise from our most intimate relations and the product of our journey through education, work, struggle and social life. However, if a person lacks reflexivity about the identifications that foster the inner voice then it can become very difficult to manage a commitment to the real 'other'. In his early years as a youth worker Steve found his job very stressful. For several years he was engaged in a struggle with a local gang for control of his club. He found it hard to stand back from this conflict, partly because he had himself been like these youths when he was their age. In other words, Steve was over-identified with the youths in his club, and to the extent that they became extensions of his self his capacity for insight into their actual difference from him was limited, inhibiting his capacity for the 'moral sensitivity' that Banks (2004) argues is necessary for welfare work. Eventually Steve was able to become less identified with them and, as this occurred, many of the misunderstandings that fuelled the conflict were overcome. Steve's early antagonists eventually became some of his most ardent supporters.

In their study of homelessness workers Miller and colleagues (Miller et al, 1995) made the useful distinction between empathic concern (the capacity to feel for the other) and emotional contagion (the capacity to feel with the other). Over-identification, as in Steve's case, draws the worker straight into the feelings of those he is working with (emotional contagion); indeed in their own research Briner and colleagues (Briner et al, 2007) found over-identification was one of the main factors contributing to stress in human services work.

Coping strategies: containing your own and others' feelings

One of the things development workers quickly learn to do is 'not to take things personally'. Among other things, those we spoke to described being attacked in public meetings, hung out to dry by local councillors, verbally and physically assaulted by angry youths. Lipsky's (1980) prescient comments on the 'assaults on the ego' of 'street-level work' seem particularly pertinent to those who work on the boundary between state and civil society.

However, with just a couple of exceptions, in a sample of 30 workers we were struck by their capacity to 'contain' their own and other's emotions. 'Containment' is a psychoanalytic term, identified by Bion (1962), describing the capacity to be affected by, holding on to and processing emotion rather than prematurely getting rid of it by acting on it or projecting it. This is an example of another youth worker talking about how he contains or manages his own feelings:

> 'I've never lost it in that aggressive sense that I just want to beat someone up or, you know, I just ... 'cos I kind of know the way young people are and that's ... you don't score any points by losing it actually. What they're really saying to you is that they want you to give ... to be very firm with them, they want you to be, you know, they want you to be solid.... And if I lose it it's a sign ... they see that as a sign of weakness.'

To contain your own and others' feelings often involves not acting precipitately. It follows that there is often a delicate balance to be struck between action and containment; indeed 'non-intervention' can be a very important way of working emotionally and relationally as we saw in our example earlier in this chapter. In contrast, Labour's modernisation agenda often appears to fetishise outputs and actions, providing little space for the emotional and relational work that is central to development interventions.

Coping strategies: combining passionate attachment with professional detachment

As noted, the emotional demands of the job seem little understood by managers or policy makers. There is a delicate balance to be struck between having a passionate attachment to the job and maintaining one's own well-being, as statistics indicating the levels of stress in occupations such as medicine and teaching reveal (Cooper and Kelly, 1993; Caplan, 1994).

Many development practitioners have deliberately chosen, in some cases for over 20 years, not to move up a career ladder in pursuit of a managerial career but to stay immersed in practice: "it's really exciting ... makes your head jump", as a health education worker described it. The importance of this often goes unnoticed even within the employing organisations, as if others see this more as an expression of a failure to move on than a positive choice. Conversely, some of those in middle management roles that we spoke to also sought to remain connected to practice, both as an essential part of keeping in touch with contemporary issues but also for the satisfaction it brought and a reminder as to why they came to work in this field.

A senior manager highlighted the importance of maintaining contact with practice:

> '... if as a manager you're not in touch with those young people through whatever route, it makes your job more difficult ... having that direct contact with ... keeps me pretty much grounded in what I'm doing really.'

Indeed, there is something about the 'aliveness of contact' that our research suggests is a value in itself, as reflected in the many incidents and experiences recounted that were funny, poignant, surprising, chaotic, exciting, moving or terrifying. These seem to perform a variety of functions – renewing energy, inspiring imagination, arousing curiosity, rekindling anger and provoking reflection and learning.

As we have seen, however, in development work, without a reflexive awareness of self, the necessary identification with 'social suffering' can become unbearable. As Sennett (2003, p 149) notes, 'respect for others can become wearing just because it would possess no limits, no boundaries'. Janice, a development worker who operates on the large public housing estate where she grew up, talks about the same issue when she speaks of her "how much do I care meter", her way of quickly measuring the amount of commitment she can afford to give to each of the different demands made by local individuals and groups she meets in the course of a typical day. Ironic detachment (Jessop, 2003) is just one of several ways in which workers struggled to preserve this necessary distance from the work.

Briner and colleagues (2007) refer to the coping technique of 'pausing and separating' as the way in which many human services workers appear to place a mental boundary around events, thereby 'not taking it home' or carrying it over from one set of work relations to another. The process of finding appropriate emotional boundaries to the work can be difficult, as illustrated by this worker speaking of the pain of separating herself from the work, making herself less approachable and providing herself with a protective shield in order to remain within a managerial role:

> 'I learned that ... it hurts too much to ... go through all the ... the nightmare of whatever your emotion is that makes people feel a kind of anger or upset or whatever.'

> [Interviewer: 'Was that difficult then to learn that?']

> 'Every day was ... it is difficult ... that way is much better than ... going home with it and ... not sleeping.... I was kind of confusing my response, a raw emotional response ... sometimes it felt personal when it actually wasn't, it was about learning to ... have that kind of boundary really ... maybe I'm not as approachable as a result....'

> [Interviewer: 'Approachable ...']

> 'To people generally, to staff, to young people ... but actually ... I don't care any more ... slightly in jest, but yeah, I do ... so if there's a downside ... that is probably it, that I'm not as ... approachable. I'm just being a bit more clear really with everybody that, where I will go and where I won't go ... I feel now much more ... aware of what I do and what I won't do.'

Having to learn that a full emotional commitment, in this case, to young people, was no longer possible or appropriate and that greater detachment was necessary represented a fundamental challenge to a sense of professional identity. Sometimes this involved the suppression of anger or guilt over the number of occasions when it was necessary to deny principles or values and conform to existing requirements.

As will be seen in Chapter Nine, the cumulative impact of modernisation processes on development work may be to encourage a greater 'emotional distancing' from the work. This appears to have paradoxical effects and produces ambivalent responses – the work becomes less stressful and facilitates a better work/life balance, but workers also become less affected by the social suffering that surrounds them. The danger is that they then become a buffer or 'thick skin', insulating government and middle-class society from the suffering in its midst.

Coping with the job: implications for training and support

Negotiating the contradictions and conflicts inherent to the development role can be an exhausting and depressing process that sucks out emotional and creative energies and involves constantly filtering out what belongs outside the work role and can be left there and what is within the work role and has to be engaged with. As we have seen, to counter such processes workers may deploy, among other strategies:

- the use of humour or irony in relation to the latest request from managers or funding bodies;
- offloading emotions with colleagues and friends;
- sustaining an intellectual critique through sharing situations and analyses (often over a drink);
- attempting to consciously keep in mind a set of values as benchmarks to measure oneself by, and monitoring the gap between one's espoused and in-use values;
- using supervision, whether managerial or non-managerial, provided this is seen as valuable;
- referring dilemmas back to the organisation through the line manager (although this was a luxury, in too many contexts, characterised by inadequate resources for supportive supervision); or
- making the dilemmas public and visible to colleagues across the sector.

One female manager described the process thus:

> 'You've got to have a lot of patience. You've got to keep
> in touch with your own vision, so against ... all the usual
> benchmarks. And be prepared to take feedback and maybe
> do things differently ... keep your eye on your vision ... and
> along the way, different things happen, and your agenda can
> change. So you have to be somehow flexible but ... and
> put that initial paperwork away in a drawer and if needed
> ... hard work, you know. You have to keep pulling people
> back in, sitting and thrashing that out.'

> [Interviewer: 'What makes you keep taking it out of the
> drawer?']

> 'That's my job, the thing to do ... I've learnt from my
> previous experience where ... you know, projects have
> been just hitting crisis points continually....'

The most important coping strategies were not those that could
be tied down to specific informal or work-based opportunities for
reflection. These professionals were coping by drawing on their own
inner resources, qualities of resilience, flexibility and creativity, rooted
in their own personal biographies, values and identities and bringing
these to the situations in hand.

There is a crucial distinction, one often lost on policy makers,
between capacities and competences/skills. To exaggerate slightly,
capacities cannot be learnt; rather, they have to be developed. One
of our respondents, at that time the chair of a CEN and deputy head
at a local comprehensive, spoke passionately about this in our final
inquiry conference. He said angrily, "there are 27 discrete skills for the
beginning teacher, and 42 for the headteacher ... training is all about
'being done to' these days". Those training interventions that state 'at
the end of this workshop you will be able to do ...' are the antithesis
of a developmental approach. The development of the capacities we
have outlined above requires a different approach, one which focuses
on the systematic supervision/mentoring of practice, learning by
observation of others and by being observed by others, working through
experience in action learning sets, inquiry groups and practice-focused
team meetings, experientially based forms of learning, and counselling,
therapy and other personal development work (Mayo et al, 2007c).

FIVE

Workers' values and commitments

More than a job

As we saw in the previous chapter, our conversations with development workers revealed a number of important insights about how they related to their work. For example, for the great majority there had not been a conscious career choice to get into development work; rather, it seemed to be more of an expression of who they were, that is, part of their identity. Moreover, many development workers had stayed committed and close to practice despite opportunities for promotion into management. It seemed that keeping in touch with practice performed a variety of functions – renewing their energy, inspiring their imagination, arousing their curiosity, rekindling their anger, provoking reflection and learning. Finally, we also noticed that it was precisely this strength of commitment to the work which often created problems as it became a source of stress, leading, for instance, to workers taking work home and threatening their ability to give time to their partner or children.

Motivation

Working in the public services is 'more than just a job'. In a survey of over 400 managers in the UK public, private and voluntary sectors, Steele (1999) found that the desire to 'benefit the community' was the most frequently cited goal of public sector managers. As she states, 'it provides a common theme and sense of purpose for people working in local government, health and the police' (1999, p 13). In contrast, managers in the private sector, for whom 'the prosperity of their organisation' was the most frequently ranked goal, ranked this objective the lowest.

The idea of different work ethics and motivations can be traced through the organisational studies literature at least as far back as Amitai Etzioni's classic study in which he contrasted what he called 'calculative' or instrumental to 'moral' forms of involvement in organisations

(Etzioni, 1961). More recently some of the same themes reappeared in Julian Le Grand's examination of motivation and agency in welfare systems (Le Grand, 2003) in which he explored the relationship between incentive systems and the promotion of altruistic as opposed to self-interested forms of human behaviour.

In *Motivation, Agency and Public Policy*, Le Grand (2003) sketched the recent history of public services in Britain in terms of a number of radical shifts. While Le Grand understands these shifts in terms of the impact of Thatcherism, it is important to understand that Thatcherism was itself just a particularly vivid example of a wider neoliberal strategy for the restructuring of the economy and society, a strategy which sought to deregulate markets and restrict the role of government in economic and public life. Le Grand argues that Thatcherism confronted deep-seated assumptions, implicit in the writings of key thinkers in British social policy of the 1960s and 1970s, such as Richard Titmuss, regarding the benign role of public service providers and the passive role of service users. In Le Grand's terms, Thatcherism challenged the view that public service workers and professionals were 'knights' and service users were 'pawns', and in its place championed the view that workers were 'knaves' and users should be 'queens' (after the private sector nostrum that the consumer is sovereign).

Le Grand defines knights as 'predominantly public-spirited or altruistic', whereas knaves he defines as 'motivated primarily by their own self-interest' (Le Grand, 2003, p 2). He recognises that more often than not public service workers are both. Later he describes 'public-spiritedness' as equivalent to 'furthering others' interests' (2003, p 13). Le Grand's analysis of motivation remains at this simplified level of altruism versus self-interest. Indeed, in later chapters of his book his analysis reverts almost entirely to economistic models of human behaviour in which agency is seen as the outcome of an individual's rationalistic and altruistic calculations. What is missing from this picture are precisely the very things that the workers in our research mentioned most frequently – the important role that their beliefs and values played in their work, the way in which their own identity as someone with, for example, a working-class or minority ethnic background influenced how they thought about society and politics, and the anger and compassion that energised them and kept them going.

Interestingly enough, although Le Grand occupies the Richard Titmuss Chair of Social Policy at the London School of Economics and Political Science, his understanding of altruism is widely at variance with Titmuss's. It is worth remembering the title, *The Gift Relationship*, of Titmuss's (1971) classic study of altruistic giving because of the way in which it gave emphasis to what is *relational*. Titmuss was indebted to the work of the anthropologist Marcel Mauss (1954). In contrast to economics, Titmuss saw the concern of social administration being with 'different types of moral transaction, embodying notions of gift exchange, of reciprocal obligations, which have developed in modern societies in institutional forms to bring about and maintain social and community relations' (Titmuss, 1968, pp 20-1). For Titmuss, common welfare is based on solidaristic interdependence. Mauss advocated what he called a morphological approach to the study of societies, that is, one concerned with the whole rather than the parts. In terms of the exchange of gifts, the focus is on the relationship not the individual. For Titmuss, following Mauss, reciprocity is not so much concerned with the maximisation of outcomes of self-interested actors but with the maintenance and reproduction of social relations themselves. As he says in a later study, social policy should be concerned with 'social growth', that is with the 'indicators that cannot be measured, cannot be quantified, but relate to the texture of relationships between human beings' (Titmuss, 1974, p 150).

Titmuss's work therefore offers a relational rather than an economistic exploration of public spiritedness, one equally relevant to the moral transactions occurring in the household, neighbourhood or the workplace as it is to the functioning of larger social systems. It enables us to see in a new light the attachments to notions of the public or community revealed by workers in studies such as Hebson et al's (2003) and Steele's (1999). Indeed, as we will see later, despite the inevitable abstractness of concepts such as 'community', many of the workers in our research expressed a strong commitment to it, alongside a concomitant anxiety that this was something that had become damaged under conditions of neoliberalism and was in need of repair.

Beyond the ethic of care

In recent years, as a result of feminist critiques of welfarism, a different way of thinking about the motivation of workers in the public and community sectors has arisen. The 'ethic of care' goes beyond earlier concepts of professional altruism by stressing the relational dimensions of the worker/citizen, carer/cared-for interaction. Instead of isolated economic actors, the ethic of care stresses their interdependence. Instead of the rational autonomous actor engaged in making choices that trade off costs and benefits to self and other, the ethic of care perspective perceives the web of reciprocal obligations and commitments that characterise relationships between helper and helped, givers and receivers. The ethic of care also highlights the affective foundation of ethical behaviour, the love and compassion that motivates moral behaviour and informs judgements about what is right and what is fair.

The concept of the ethic of care was not just an antidote to naïve notions of altruism that had characterised earlier forms of professional self-justification; it also challenged prevailing assumptions in politics about concepts of justice. Within traditional political theory justice had been seen as synonymous with impartiality. Principles of justice were arrived at through processes of reasoned argument that abstracted away from the particular lives and needs of individuals and groups towards universal principles that were held to be applicable to all cases and instances. As noted in Chapter Two, such 'impartialist' models of ethics were challenged by feminists who stressed that in real life what was right and good was inevitably contingent to the particular relationship that a teacher, nurse or community worker was engaged in. Universal principles had their place but could not act as a guide to workers engaged in face-to-face relationships with needy, angry or vulnerable others. In such face-to-face encounters what was fair was not usually obvious as workers were often faced with conflicting needs and claims and were engaged in complex relations of authority and power (Thompson and Hoggett, 1996). Michael Lipsky, in a landmark study of the work of the police, magistrates, social workers and others, referred to such conflicts as the dilemmas of the street-level bureaucrat (1980).

The ethic of care, in contrast, offered a partialist model of ethics (Banks, 2004, pp 98-104), one that stressed the complexity of actual relationships rather than abstract principles and rules. More recently, in her stimulating analysis of the ethic of care, Selma Sevenhuijsen (1998) carefully sets out to detach care from its gendered affiliations. She notes how care is a crucial dimension of all aspects of life, not just the intimate and familial. She also questions the value of the care/justice dichotomy and the female/partial versus male/impartial binary on which this has become grounded. Whereas partialist models emphasise the situated and relational aspects of ethical behaviour, impartialist models stress the importance of abstract and universal principles. We suggest that this line of inquiry could be taken further.

In a section of her book entitled 'justice and solidarity', Sevenhuijsen (1998, pp 144-5) notes:

> It remains important to remember that the care–justice dichotomy is at its sharpest when justice is framed in the

epistemological parameters of the paradigm of distributive justice, in which abstract rationality, impartiality and sameness are paramount. If we base our moral arguments, instead, on social practices and an explicit awareness of the way these are affected by power and domination, we may be able to arrive at enriched notions of justice.

But we believe that in terms of people's actual lived lives it is not only care or compassion that has an affective basis but also the commitment to social justice. For just as love and reparation constitute the affective dimension of care, so anger and a sense of grievance constitute the affective basis of the commitment to social justice. Indeed, what seems to emerge from our interviews is the way in which a complex mix of compassion and anger fuels a reparative desire to undo the damage and suffering experienced by particular groups or communities or, in Titmuss's terms, a desire to repair the texture of social relations. This seems to us more like solidarity (Hoggett, 2006) than altruism. As Sevenhuijsen (1998, p 147) notes, 'the notion of solidarity gives a political meaning to care and to mutual commitment'. We suggest that this affective aspect of the commitment to care and social justice corresponds to an enduring moral sentiment.

Anger and injustice

For several decades now, political sociologists have been concerned to understand the factors that contribute to or undermine struggles for social justice. Why is it that sometimes the experience of injustice leads to political mobilisation whereas on other occasions it does not? The early phases of this approach focused on the resources like finance, information and organisational capability, whose availability to activists appeared to make the movement from grievance to action more likely (McCarthy and Zald, 1977). Later approaches focused on what became known as the 'political opportunity structure'. In the work of Sidney Tarrow (1994) and Doug McAdam and colleagues (McAdam et al, 1996) contextual factors such as the existence of fractures and cleavages within dominant political elites not only strongly influenced whether political mobilisation occurred or not but also the nature of the tactics that activists were likely to use. There has, in addition, been an increasing focus on what the activists could do themselves to change the situation they faced. David Snow and Robert Benford (Snow et al, 1986; Snow and Benford, 1988) argued for the importance of 'ideational factors', and analysed the ideological work of movement organisers and activists in terms of a theory of 'frame alignment'. This approach focused on the meanings, values and ideas that are the currency of political action, something traditionally conceived of by activists in terms of 'consciousness raising' or 'conscientisation'.

More recently, this desire to understand the contribution of activists' own agency has also led to an interest in the role of emotions and identities in movement mobilisation and demobilisation. Axel Honneth (1995) links injustice to social conflict through his concept of 'struggles for recognition'. For Honneth, there is a universal need for all individuals and groups to be loved, respected and esteemed. Without love the basic existential security that citizens require in order to engage with others on the basis of trust is absent. Without respect people are construed as somehow deficient as citizens capable of engaging in public life and as a consequence they are denied access to full civil, economic and social rights, just as women and black people in Western democracies were once denied the vote and many other basic rights. Without esteem a group feels that its way of life is not valued by the society that it belongs to, that its values, lifestyle, religion or mores are somehow inferior. Honneth argues that lack of recognition leads to different forms of hurt – humiliation, disrespect and denigration. These different forms of hurt produce both grief (from a sense of loss) and grievance (anger towards the perpetrators of such hurt), and it is these emotions that fuel political struggles to rectify such injustice.

Honneth links the experience of injustice to group identity and the struggle for respect, but there are many other sources for the emotions that drive political struggles for justice. James Jasper offers an alternative perspective through his concept of 'moral shocks' (Jasper, 1998):

> "Moral shocks", often the first step toward recruitment into social movements, occur when an unexpected event or piece of information raises such a sense of outrage in a person that she becomes inclined toward political action, whether or not she has acquaintances in the movement. (Jasper, 1998, p 409)

Jasper argues that in some situations moral shocks propel individuals directly into political action even in the absence of mediating networks of workmates, friends or family (Jasper and Poulsen, 1995).

Struggles for recognition and moral shocks find expression in what Gamson (1992) called 'injustice frames'. These have both cognitive and affective dimensions. Regarding the former, Gamson and his colleagues connect such frames to an interpretation of events that suggest that an authority system is violating the shared moral principles of participants to those events. Referring to the latter Gamson speaks of 'the righteous anger that puts fire in the belly and iron in the soul' (Gamson, 1992). From this brief excursion into political sociology we can see an alternative approach to conceptualising injustice. Rather than the abstract and rational ruminations of political philosophers, here is a tradition which understands that justice is inseparable from struggle and conflict and the anger and outrage which fuels the political action of subaltern groups.

Solidarity: angry compassion

Values are centrally important to development workers, both to those with middle-class backgrounds and to those who have come to the work through their own personal history of struggle in poor or marginalised communities. This commitment to values emerged among the unpaid development workers who were interviewed, in parallel, as part of the CDF/SCCD study. There was a strong allegiance in many interviewees, this report concluded, to the value of community, social justice and the importance of working with community members. These values were clearly defined and there was an overall, 'idealism or belief system about community involvement that was clear and distinct from personal motivations, perhaps for social contact or personal interests in a particular area' (Gaffney, 2002, p 8). Typically for these unpaid workers, this commitment – often fuelled by personal experiences of social injustices and/or poor local conditions or services – led them from one form of involvement to another.

Personal biographies and injustice

In our conversations with development workers we realised that a variety of different values and motivations underlay their commitment to what they did. We also began to realise how deeply held these were, how frequently earlier life experiences had nurtured a sensitivity to injustice and the compassion and anger that accompanied this. For some this was based on personal injustices that had befallen them. For example, Isobel had never formally trained as a youth or community worker but came to it through many years of community and political action. However, she was also very clear about the impact of her own troubled adolescence while never being completely explicit about what she went through:

'I had a very unhappy adolescence and a very painful adolescence and so I think that was one of the things that brought me to working with teenagers definitely, because the adults outside my family at that time were very, very important to me ... and I think the sort of campaigning part is also a part that I think for a lot of people and for me is ... I don't know ... at some level, on an emotional level, about advocating for bits that are in pain, you know, just damaged.'

For others, this was linked to their experience of the injustices that had befallen close family members. Sandra grew up in an old Commonwealth country where her father was a civil engineer. As she put it:

'I grew up in a family where my mum was much the stronger figure and was quite critical in all sorts of ways about my dad ... I think she'd grown up in a sort of aspiring middle class ... [dad] was always made, I suppose by my mother, to feel that, you know, just try and be a bit better.'

Even in her early school days Sandra was conscious of those who, in her words, "missed out" and, in the interview, she connected this to the way in which she identified with her criticised father. Later, at university, she found herself developing a lifelong interest in "people who were disadvantaged about their learning" as opposed to some of her fellow students who she referred to as "smug young women". Thirty years on and Sandra still dedicates her career to education work with manual workers through partnerships her organisation has created with trade unions such as Unison.

Very often this experience of injustice was linked to class or 'race'. Jan grew up on a public housing estate in a large city:

'... my dad was, he was an odd mixture of kind of Italian macho and very masculine, and being completely cowed by the world as well. He knew his place and he accepted his place and would never argue his place ... my mum was a waitress for years and years, and my dad used to come and pick her up from work. And she said you'd watch him walking through the restaurant and she said the only people who went in restaurants in those days were people in suits and people with money, you know, that was in the sixties.

She said you'd watch him walk through the restaurant,
she said, and he was almost physically shrinking as he was
walking through, because he didn't belong.'

Jan's mum was the complete opposite, proud of her class and cynical
towards the pretensions of those with money and power. Jan admitted
to having both a bit of her mum and her dad in her, but it was her
mum that she drew on in her unshakeable desire to strengthen the
voice of communities like the one she had grown up in.

Cass, a black community worker, had been orphaned as a child
and grew up in the care system. She became a victim of some of the
abusive regimes that existed in children's homes in the early 1970s and
suffered different forms of abuse within the care system. There was
much less understanding of the importance of listening to children in
care then; indeed, she was blamed for bringing the trouble on herself.
This experience still provides a powerful motivation for her work now.
As Cass put it:

'All those things I'm sure have had an impact on me in
saying that I don't actually want anybody else to be in a
position where their voice isn't heard. I'm sure it's about
that. I'm sure that's where all this is coming from.'

In her twenties and out of the care system Cass soon became involved
in the struggle of the Afro-Caribbean community of Brixton against
the police and other authorities. For Cass the unheard voice of the
abused child in care soon joined with the unheard voice of the black
people of south London in their struggle against institutional racism.

A reparative impulse

The anger at injustice is connected to a desire to change things, to
improve the conditions of people's lives, to make things better. Our
research suggests that the strong sense of emotional commitment felt
by development workers was often rooted in a 'reparative impulse'
manifest in the desire to help repair damaged communities, help
troubled individuals and families and/or empower those who did
not have a voice. What is crucial is the way in which this reparative
impulse becomes connected to broader notions of group solidarity and
anger at injustice; it is therefore something very different to simple
altruism. For many participants, this impulse found expression in a
passionate desire to undo some of the damage that has been done to

others, for example, to the lives of young people or to neglected and misunderstood communities.

Some traced the strength of this impulse to their own experiences of injustice and hardship as a young person and a desire not to let what happened to them happen to others. For example, although Steve's parents were both professionals they also had such severe addiction problems that by the age of 11 Steve had been placed into state care. Looking back at that time and the absence of someone who could have supported him, he lamented the absence of:

> '... someone who could have understood what a young person goes through ... who's having problems at home, no one to listen to him, no one really cares where they're going or what they're doing.'

For Steve, that kind of person remains very special to him and, through the interview process, Steve became very aware it was his desire to be this kind of figure that now motivated him as a youth worker on an isolated outer city estate.

Stef began her life history interview by saying that from about the age of 13 she had wanted to be a social worker:

> 'I actually had no real idea of what that was or what that meant or anything, really, if I'm honest, it was just a name and a tag. There were significant things that made me think I wanted to do that. I had an experience where, at 13, where I just thought I wanted to speak to an adult that wasn't my parents but I had none ... I didn't have anybody to talk to and I felt very alone and very scared ... I don't want anybody to ever feel like I feel now.'

Stef's slip of the tongue in the last sentence (she says "feel now" rather than "felt then") indicates how she, as with Isobel and Steve, still identifies with the troubled child that she once was. For Isobel there was also the experience of a good authority figure that would listen to her, whereas for Stef this absent figure became established inside her as an ideal, someone she aspired to become. All three identified deeply with young people and in advocating for this group they were advocating, as Isobel put it, for that part of them that was still in pain.

Sylvia's parents were both qualified general practitioners (GPs). But this was the 1950s, when a woman's proper role was in the home. By all accounts Sylvia's mother, who had a rural Irish Roman Catholic background, took very unhappily to giving up her job for motherhood and Sylvia describes going to boarding school at the tender age of seven as both profoundly painful but also a "great relief". In those early years she reflected, "The best times were always when my dad was around". Her mother was a very difficult woman, "We could never understand why she was so often grumpy ... it was only later that we began to realise what she missed out on". But at a certain point her mother could take no more:

> 'The Pope's encyclical really enraged her, about contraception ... she joined the Family Planning Association ... and that was her saving grace really, it made such a difference 'cos she found something useful to do, positive to do that she believed in.'

After leaving university Sylvia became involved in the Women's Movement and, while still in her early twenties, she met a group of women in north London who were "high flying really sort of professional women but they were looking after small children at the time and they wanted a local childcare campaign". The work of this group of women has been an enduring ideal for Sylvia, and not surprisingly because they represented all that at times she felt her mother was not able to realise during Sylvia's childhood. Throughout her working life Sylvia's community work has focused on the needs of young women and particularly young mothers.

In all these examples we can see how a young person's reparative impulse becomes linked to an identification with the troubled aspects of a parent and how the desire to make things better for the parent, in adult life, later becomes displaced from the individual to a group – educationally disadvantaged adults, women looking after children.

Valuing community and democracy

For others in our sample their commitment to the 'public interest' (Pratchett and Wingfield, 1996) and a desire to 'benefit the community' (Steele, 1999) seemed more evidently rooted in the strength of the values surrounding them in early life, from religious faith for example and/or from political, trade union and labour movement commitments. For several participants it was a good experience, internalised as a benign presence that formed the basis of their adult identities. For many some deeply ingrained notion of community, despite different understandings, was a key value. Stuart had a working-class background and was immersed in labour movement activism and extended networks, which he described as "a loving environment". One of five siblings, his father died when he was 16, but Stuart felt that he had received a lot of support from his mother and "both my mum's sisters and my father's brothers, so I never felt we were a lone parent [family]". As a deputy head of an inner-city comprehensive school, Stuart's commitment extends beyond the school gates to fighting for the community from which his pupils are drawn:

> 'I regard the children and the families here as my people. The kind of people I grew up with and deserve the best chance … I was only one boy in my primary school that went to grammar school. But I want to create those opportunities here for every boy and girl who comes.'

Gus grew up in a northern mining family, one with a tradition of trade union involvement. But it was also a family that allowed him to make his own choices – not to go from school to university even though he could have done so and, later in his twenties, to give up a well-paid management job to go into youth work. For Gus, this family experience formed his deep commitment to a democratic community. As he put it:

> 'I have a strong view and values, value system based upon people's choice, the right to choose, and I think people, given the proper support, can make decisions for themselves … I'm a great, I'm a big supporter of … of, I guess what we'd call democracy, true 'd', true 'd', true democracy.'

As someone holding a senior position in a city's youth service it was this value that guided the philosophy behind his work. For Gus and Stuart 'community' seemed to have been incorporated as an extension of a good early family environment, a benign presence now inside themselves, part of their inner world, the source of a strong set of values providing guidance without being prescriptive. This commitment to values also emerged among the unpaid workers interviewed in the SCCD survey. There was a strong allegiance in many interviewees to the value of community, social justice and the importance of working with community members. These values were clearly defined and there was an overall idealism or belief system about community involvement that was clear and distinct, from 'personal motivations, perhaps for social contact or personal interests in a particular area' (Gaffney, 2002, p 8).

Typically for these unpaid workers, this commitment – often fuelled by personal experiences of social injustices and/or poor local conditions/ services – led them from one form of involvement to another. In our research, both the very experienced and relative newcomers spoke, often passionately, about their values and how these were central to their professional identities. Typical comments included:

> 'I'd like to say that I've contributed to my community.'

> 'This stuff is about social justice and that's one of the things that motivate me.'

> 'There is something to be done in terms of serving people here in this job ... I'm idealistic.'

One experienced manager noted that he had spent 28 years developing a professional work practice and that while such principles had developed and grown, they remained rooted in the same basic values of social justice:

> 'I'm quite fierce about what I believe to be in the community – the rights and responsibilities of people to be treated with respect and supported to make the right choices.'

This 'respect for individuals and communities', as reiterated by a much younger community entrepreneur, was shared by many, even though they often recognised that they did not necessarily have a clear overall ethical framework worked out in detail. However articulated, these basic values, together with the satisfaction gained from aspects of the job, sustained motivation. Without a set of beliefs about things, it was suggested:

> 'I don't think you could do this kind of work ... something's going to have to carry you through.'

These early identifications with, for example, parents, grandmothers, uncles, teachers and care workers, also appear to play a key role in shaping social identities, that is, in the way our participants 'became' black, female or working class. Such identities cannot be separated from values. Participants talked about values in very concrete terms, both as a clear set of principles but also as something very practical. Such connections provide the foundation on which more overtly political values that stress mutuality and solidarity have been built.

For Larry, in contrast, community was something he discovered late, and was about finding an identity. Larry's family survived the holocaust but as refugees living in London they kept very much to themselves. Larry was aware of strong and thriving Jewish communities around him but as a child he was left to make his own connections to it. It was only in his twenties, after marriage, that he speaks of "joining a Jewish community". For Larry this sense of community has obviously been enormously important in redressing the isolation he felt during his childhood. In the early interviews he often spoke of "the social glue" which he found in this faith community, and this has clearly been a crucial underlying motivation in guiding him through a series of jobs in the private sector towards his then current role where he was directing an inner-city community regeneration project.

From the personal to the political

Such experiences and associated values appeared to act as the foundation on which more overtly political values were built, such as those that stressed mutuality and solidarity. Education and professional training added further to this foundation, but the foundation enabled practitioners to bring their own personal meanings to these systems of ideas. We were struck by how many practitioners had been heavily involved in political activism (very broadly defined) before coming into their present work – through experiences at university, trade union work and through engagement in wider political struggles. For some this may have contributed as much to their education as obtaining a degree or undertaking professional training. In this respect age is a factor since the 'political education' of those who, for example, experienced the emergence of the women's liberation movement, struggles against the impact of Thatcherism, the Scarman Inquiry and miners' strikes would be different to those who 'cut their teeth' on animal liberation, the Stephen Lawrence Inquiry and the emergence of the anti-globalisation movement. Such differences regarding both specific events and the context in which they occurred are likely to affect the ways in which generations think about the meaning of 'public'.

Many of our sample therefore had personal experiences of injustice to self or to others that provided the foundation for their later commitments. For the majority of the development workers who had working-class or ethnic minority backgrounds, their own later experiences as users of welfare services provided the bridge into activism. As youths, some of our sample would themselves have been considered 'at risk of offending' in today's professional jargon. Jim grew up in Docklands during the 1980s when traditional industries and much public housing were collapsing all around him. "As kids it was brilliant ... we used to go into these houses and knock 'em down, that was like our fun, knocking these houses down." Jim recounts burning down boarded-up housing: "... we were the horrible young men of the Beaufort Estate...". Like the youths in Paul Willis's (1978) classic study of young working-class men, Jim and his friends liked "having a larf", and, like all his friends, Jim loathed school:

> 'The teachers who were the most vicious and bullying, and the same with police or anyone else in authority, we provoke 'em, make 'em cane ya and then laugh at them.... Their authority disappears very quickly after that and they tend to leave you alone.'

But Jim eventually came across some good authority figures, adventure playground workers, "we used to make their lives a bit miserable ... but we used to work with them and they'd change us a bit". It didn't deter them from burning down the adventure playground building, however. Jim continued:

> 'I'd go to the youth club, St Stephens which is still there ... we used to get in trouble there an' all because people used to ask us to do things we didn't wanna do and stuff ... and eventually someone just turned around and said, "Jim, instead of just moaning about this place why don't you just come and do something".'

And he did, he started doing voluntary youth work, eventually got some GCSEs and A-levels and ended up doing a youth and community work course at university. His formal education complemented his informal education and his youthful delinquency became political militancy expressed in anti-fascist work and trade union organising.

For some of the women in our sample it was their role as carers that brought them into activism. For Yvonne, another black community worker in our sample, it was her struggle to ensure that her daughter got a good education in the face of institutional racism in schools that galvanised her, particularly when she realised how little things had moved on since her own unsatisfactory experiences as a black London schoolgirl. For Carol, a white development worker operating in the working-class community where she had grown up, it was her experience of her children's teachers' low expectations that first got her involved in activism.

For many of the development workers in our sample who had more middle-class backgrounds their activism tended to emerge during the more familiar journey involved in leaving home, going to college or university and then becoming involved in a range of activities in political, community and/or voluntary organisations. The nature of the involvement tended to reflect the nature of the period – for several older workers it was the women's movement of the 1970s that was formative; for some of the younger workers it was squatting and animal rights in the late 1980s and early 1990s that was crucial. While none in our sample regretted these involvements, some did now look back on them with a degree of self-criticism. While their commitment to overcoming injustices remained undaunted, they appeared to have a greater appreciation that power relations sometimes did not make themselves present in simple, black and white, ways. Our respondents, many previously active in the new social movements, impressed us by the depth of their ethical reasoning and feeling. As we shall see in Chapter Six, many of them had a firm set of values, held in a non-idealised way, which provided orientation in dilemmatic space.

Solidarity and criticism

We have argued that it is more useful to think of the development workers' commitment to the job as one based on solidarity rather than altruism. Altruism can imply an asymmetrical relationship between one who gives and one who receives, between someone who has agency and someone who lacks it. Much of the 'empowerment' model can be considered in this light. Couched still in terms of the deficit model – particularly a deficit of agency – the welfare citizen becomes an object of empowerment strategies. Empowerment, like community, becomes construed as something poor people lack, a fundamentally patronising model of development. The point is well made by the following interview with Jim, a local activist in south London who had become a professional youth and community worker and who has been heavily involved in recent Labour regeneration strategies targeted at neighbourhoods such as the one he had grown up in:

> 'I mean how can anyone look themselves in the eye, in the eye in the morning and then go out to work and say they're building people's capacity ... it defeats me, seriously. It's no

more different isn't it than crude bloody learning, you know,
pour bad ideas out, pour good ones back in again.'

As noted earlier, Jim had been a bit of a handful as a teenager. As
an active trade unionist Jim now found his early encounters with
authority invaluable: "I've been reasonably good at sniffing out power
and sniffing out the flaws in power and how to undermine it". In the
early 1990s when the service he worked for was threatened with major
cutbacks, he led a strike that threw him into a personal confrontation
with his employer. He took enormous risks with the lives of the trade
union members he led and, at times, engaged in pure brinkmanship.
But the employers blinked first and backed down. As he put it, "they
rely on their authority and they rely on people's innate fear". He feels
that he learnt from his schooldays that if you show no fear, authority
crumbles.

Because Jim sees himself in the children he now works with he knows
that he has to use his own authority carefully otherwise he will just
provoke the same kind of reaction he had when teachers and youth
workers tried to tell him what he could and could not do:

> 'I came to the kinda conclusion ... that if that's how I got
> where I was and I could do that instinctively, it was likely
> that people brought up in similar circumstances would do
> it, so actually I don't set up a power dynamic, don't tell
> 'em what to do ... 'cos they'll be so frigged by someone
> saying don't ... so like anywhere I've worked people are
> allowed to drink if they want, smoke weed if they want ...
> I wanna have conversations with these people no matter
> what they do.'

Jim steadfastly insists on not being judgemental:

> 'There is nothing wrong, there is nothing ethically, morally
> or structurally wrong with the way they choose to live their
> lives ... if you allow people to talk and you take what they
> are saying seriously and they think you are ... the kind of
> things people are up for chatting about and sorting are just,
> I think actually quite humbling, given the circumstances in
> which people have to live their lives.'

So, as he sees it, Jim seeks to achieve a relationship of mutual respect,
one that recognises that young people have problems but rejects the

idea that they *are* a problem. Yet, while nearly all of the workers in our sample rejected the idea that young people or poor people were a problem or were deficient in some way, they nevertheless had different views about what respecting the other implied. Did it, for example, mean that you should not challenge the behaviour or views of the other if they disrespected you or others? For Jim, when young people broke the rules by bringing weed onto the premises, they were not challenging him personally, they were challenging authority, just as he had when he was their age. But what happens when a worker is confronted by young people's involvement in violent gangs, or by local residents who repeatedly put down and intimidate others in committee meetings, or by local activists who are brilliant organisers and fearless campaigners but who are also prejudiced against members of minority groups living in their area? In these kind of situations is it possible to be both respectful towards the other and critical?

Here is another example from our research. Despite being subject to physical attack on several occasions, having his staff abused, and seeing children he knows becoming addicts or prostitutes, Si retained a stubborn capacity to see some good in even the most desperate and ugly children – even one who attacked him and ended up in jail. He spoke eloquently about this when describing his feelings on seeing the pictures of several youths, some of whom he knew well, who had been subject to Anti-Social Behaviour Orders (ASBOs) for their violent and disorderly behaviour on the housing estate where they lived:

> 'Last week I saw all the shops around here have mug shots of the 10 most difficult young people and I was at a meeting of the shopkeepers and I saw these, sort of, rows of photographs and they're a very desperate bunch. I mean, I was probably the only person in the room who knew all the people and it's just very sad to see this. I know they're dangerous ... but there is just a feeling of, is this the right way, but I can't think of another way. You know, I can't think of another way of getting these people out of their desperation. I mean, what struck me most about them is that they are a very unloved group, but all we can offer them is disciplinary, um, sort of, measures against them. We can't actually offer them love. It would be asking too much of us.... My main feeling is, yes, they just have absolutely no love in their lives at all and all we're doing is punishing them more and more. It feels, kind of, wrong.'

Si felt totally conflicted about this, recognising that they were a 'bad bunch' but also feeling genuine compassion for them, accepting that they were dangerous but also seeing the vulnerability in their violence, wanting to do something but not knowing what and yet also being aware that he was colluding with their suppression. Si accepted that these youths could be nasty and something needed to be done. But he did not see them as irredeemable and it is because he still had this hope that he found the picture of the mug shots so painful. He just about managed to retain some kind of hopefulness because he could still see the good within the bad. He did not oppose the ASBOs on principle like some might, yet he also felt that they were not the solution, but he did not know what the solution was (and probably believed that there was no solution).

Accepting the badness of the youths' behaviour did not in any way undermine his sense of the injustice of it all; if anything it strengthened this. For he could see how, in subtle ways, people got destroyed inside by the world in which they lived, and this made him all the more angry. But he also knew that these young people could have acted differently for he knew many of their friends, and not all of them had taken the same path. He therefore felt angry for them and angry at them. It was not a question of either/or, but one of both/and.

SIX

Negotiating dilemmatic space

Contested space

We made a distinction in previous chapters between those challenges that are inherent to the role of development workers, operating as they do on the boundary of state and civil society, and those which have arisen more specifically in the context of Labour's modernisation agenda. As we shall see in more detail in Chapter Eight, the modernisation agenda (Newman, 2001) has created its own dilemmas for such workers. The emphasis on short-term outputs and 'measurables', the heightened competition for time-limited funding streams (referred to as 'troughing' in some parts of the voluntary sector), the bureaucratic demands of project management work and the positivist and rationalistic ethos that now underlies much evidence-based practice and competence-based models of professional development leads to a managerialisation of welfare practice (Halford and Leonard, 1999, 2005) from which development workers are not immune. There is a real tension, revealed by our research, between these initiatives and the values of the development profession with its emphasis on long-term and sustainable change, outcomes rather than outputs, relationships and processes as well as activities.

In the previous two chapters we began to hypothesise a set of factors – human capacities, values, identities, social networks, institutional environments, discursive practices – which provide the conditions for ethical agency in this contested space. Each factor is potentially both a resource and a constraint. For example, the personal identity of a worker formed out of unique biographical circumstances and from the formations of class, 'race' and gender provides resources to be drawn on but also limits that person's sense of what is possible or desirable (Hoggett, Beedell, Jimenez, Mayo and Miller, 2006). Professionals bring something to their role in terms of values, identities and emotional capacities that pre-exist their engagement in that role. In this sense, the subject always partly precedes discourse and, far from being the simple bearer of a discourse such as modernisation, also has the capacity to resist it (Halford and Leonard, 2005).

Values are important in a second way. It became clear to us that many in our sample used their values as a kind of compass in dilemmatic space. We now realise that we are in the territory of Charles Taylor's (1989) work, as Taylor argues that values provide us with what he calls 'orientation' in moral space.

Capacities of the 'capacity builders'

In Chapter One we introduced the concept of human capacities, arguing that they referred to fluid potentialities in contrast to Martha Nussbaum's notion of 'capabilities'. Of course, with the progressive managerialisation of governance we find today that the dominant concepts of human attributes are even more fixed – the idea of 'competences' that can be measured in terms of tangible indicators, for example, now carries enormous weight.

In contrast we suggest that the negotiation of dilemmatic space constitutes a challenge to our capacity to contain complexity. In an extended examination of the idea of 'capacity', Robert French (1999) notes the etymology of this word, its derivation from the Latin *capac*, meaning 'able to take in' or 'able to hold much'. Under the conditions of contemporary modernity the question is, how much of the complexity of everyday life is it possible to take in, and how much of this reality can be faced? The question is both a political and a personal one because the dilemmas provoked by living in a complex world generate and connect to internal conflicts within us. Development work confronts individuals with a range of dilemmas that are particularly acute for, as we have seen, this role puts workers in that contested space between government and civil society. One example, drawn from our research, is illustrative of this point.

Eunice created and led a children and families project that was highly embedded in the multicultural neighbourhood where she lived. The project was immersed in the local social networks of the surrounding area. Local black people not only used its services, they were its volunteers and management committee members and some had become members of staff. One such member of staff, someone with whom Eunice identified strongly because of what he had managed to survive in his own life, crossed the line in terms of what was acceptable professional behaviour:

> 'It was about his, you know, lack of understanding of youth work, the boundaries and how, it's this thing of employing, in many ways he had good qualities for the job but he wasn't a

professionally trained youth worker and he brought some of
his old kinda street stuff into his work too much. And, and,
but couldn't see that, couldn't see that that was a problem.
Thought he was being victimised....'

When confronted by Eunice he refused to acknowledge that he had
made a serious mistake. The worker had a strong reputation in the local
community and was well liked by many members of staff and service
users. After much agonising, Eunice decided to instigate disciplinary
procedures against him. To make matters even more complex, the man
was then represented by a solicitor who was also a close friend of Eunice
and this put a strain on her friendship as "she was supporting somebody
who I thought was being extremely unreasonable". Moreover, the
man's partner was friends with other members of staff and his child
used the day nursery, and so, while disciplinary action was being taken,
these other kinds of relationships were still going on. To make matters
worse, the man concerned kept putting his case to people he knew in
the local community "saying that we were unfair ... because we have
got a really good reputation on the community, I didn't want that to
be tainted". Eunice continued to hope that her colleague would see
sense and at least come and talk to her about the issue, but he did not
back down. Eventually he resigned before the disciplinary could be
pursued through to its conclusion, something that Eunice reacted to
with both relief and sadness.

The project operated on the boundaries between state and civil
society and Eunice was therefore subject to the demands both of the
formal and impersonal rules and procedures of government and of the
informal, person-to-person relations of civil society. This contradiction
was exacerbated by policies that on the one hand stressed the importance
of local involvement and local job creation and on the other gave
expression to an increasingly 'risk conscious' and 'risk averse' culture
(Cooper and Lousada, 2005), particularly where young people were
involved (Ferguson, 2004). Eunice identified with professional standards
and ethics that claimed to be universal in applicability but suspected
these were gendered and racialised and that her colleague's behaviour
was not necessarily unacceptable – at least within sections – within
his own community. It was very rare, indeed almost unprecedented,
for a white woman to lead a community project in this district and
she ran the risk of being ostracised by the local black community for
disciplining this popular local activist. Thus Eunice was caught between
the conflicting claims of bureaucracy and civil society, universalism
and multiculturalism, class and 'race'. In telling us that she agonised

over what to do, Eunice described the 'emotion work' involved in negotiating these kinds of ethical dilemmas (Hoggett, 2005b).

Our research suggests that there are a variety of ways of traversing dilemmatic space. As Eunice did, we can accept our mixed and contradictory feelings, contain our ambivalence but act *for the best*, recognising that even if the risk of catastrophe can be averted the outcome will inevitably be messy and painful. Jessop (2003), reflecting on the complexity of the coordination problem now facing the task of governance, argues that there is not just a risk of failure but that 'failure' is inherent to the work of government. He advocates the stance of the 'romantic ironist' who 'accepts incompleteness and failure as essential features of social life but continues to act as if completeness and success were possible' (Jessop, 2003, p 109). However one chooses to react, what is clear is that such stances require a considerable capacity to contain loss and disappointment. As Mendus (2000) notes, the impossibility of harmonious reconciliation means that the moral agent is not exempt from the authority of the claim she chooses to reject and suggests that such situations are characterised by 'pluralism, plus conflict, plus loss' (2000, p 117).

What then happens to individuals who cannot bear the frustrations and disappointments that inevitably attend the lives of those committed to providing public services? Our research suggests that it can quickly lead to demoralisation. Either the individual internalises a sense of failure so that s/he becomes depressed and despairing or s/he projects these failings onto those seen as responsible for these frustrations – the state, the public, the community and so on. If Eunice had internalised this sense of failure she would have ended up feeling bad; if she had projected it onto others she would probably have begun to feel that 'the community' had betrayed her. In our experience, public service workers including development workers often experience loss and disappointment in terms of personal failure, particularly in a political environment in which bureaucrats and welfare workers are easy scapegoats for public problems. It is as if they internalise the flaws and failings of society thereby taking responsibility for what is irresolvable in the wider world.

Returning to French's reflections on human capacities, he notes how the concept has quietly become a consistent preoccupation of those groupings within psychoanalysis influenced by the work of Klein, Winnicott and Bion (see Symington, 1986). Klein describes two contrasting ways of apprehending the world that differ in the degree of complexity they can hold. From what she calls the 'paranoid schizoid' position, reality is dealt with by splitting, fragmenting, compartmentalising and other means of simplification, each of which requires a separating out of good and bad, virtue and vice, purity and contamination. We can see how both forms of demoralisation (self-blame and other-blame) express this position. In contrast, Klein describes another state of mind she refers to as the 'depressive position' in which, as with Eunice, the possibility that things may be more 'mixed up' (including one's own feelings and motives) can be entertained. Klein uses the word 'depressive' not because the person in this state of mind is depressed but as a way of acknowledging the sadness and remorse that accompanies recognition of the complexity of life and of one's own and others' failings. Perhaps a more accessible term for this state of mind would be Neville Symington's alternative phrase, the 'tragic position' (Symington, 1986). In dilemmatic space things often do not work out as we would like or hope and everyday life often has a slightly tragic quality to it, as Eunice found out to her cost. As Sidney Hook once put it, 'faced by problems, nothing is better than thoughtful action, but our best actions may not be enough. We cannot escape risk because even an informed choice may be an unlucky one' (Hook, 1974, p 59). As Freud always insisted, facing reality requires a toughmindedness. Instead of an idealisation of one's self and one's group, in the tragic or depressive position there is a more realistic appreciation of the bad within the good (that is my/our faults, weaknesses, limitations), and instead of a denigration of the other there is a more generous appreciation of the good within the bad (including the strengths of other value systems to our own).

If, as has been argued, 'dilemmatic space' poses a challenge to our ethical capacities then the tragic position seems to be a response to this challenge, for without the capacity to adopt this position we are unable to handle the dilemmas of modern life. Yet if this provides us with a clue regarding the psychical resources needed to contain the complexity of modern life, it may not yet give us an answer to how effective agency is possible. A correlate of the tragic or depressive position is the ability to take the position of the other, including the other who stands as opponent or antagonist to self. If Eunice lacked this capacity she would have remained unaffected by the competing claims of class and culture represented by her black colleague and to this extent the multifaceted nature of the dilemma she was in would have eluded her grasp. However, our research, particularly the interviews with several other women in our sample, indicated that the ability to take the position of the other, to surrender to competing claims, could be paralysing. It can lead to inaction and indecision, to an agonised impotence. In contrast, Eunice could combine such openness to experience with the capacity for decisive action. There was a sense of authority to her that some others in her situation lacked. The question therefore remains, what additional internal resources are required to steer a course in the ambiguous, contested and uncertain terrain of dilemmatic space? Our research suggests that in order to do so an individual needs to be self-authorising. This is discussed more fully in the next chapter but suffice to say here that by this we mean the sense of authority or belief in oneself that the person brings to their own agency. We can think of this in terms of the presence or absence of an authoritative internal voice that an individual can draw on but a voice constructed from a matrix of identifications with significant others.

Values: orientation in moral space

We have argued that contemporary capitalist social relations on a global scale confront the individual with unprecedented social complexity. On the one hand social relations become increasingly pluralised and on the other the exercise of power, including the power of the state (Burrows and Loader, 1994), becomes increasingly remote and obscured. Condemned to freedom in this dilemmatic space the individual requires both a capacity to contain complexity and a sense of inner authority to be able to act with integrity. They also require strong values. Concepts of value and value pluralism have become familiar enough in political philosophy, particularly since the work of Isaiah Berlin, but even here, as Charles Taylor (1989) notes, there has been an over-emphasis on the right (one's obligations, what one ought to do) and an under-emphasis on the good (one's ideals and values).

As an object of analysis and empirical investigation in politics, sociology and psychoanalysis, values (as opposed to beliefs, discourses, etc) remain even more neglected. Take psychoanalysis for example. Since Freud the attention of psychoanalysis has been fixed firmly on the role of the super-ego as the mediator of the moral precepts of succeeding generations and yet such precepts hardly constitute 'values' in the way in which we normally think about them. In normal usage values, particularly those Raz (2003, p 34) refers to as enabling or facilitating values such as freedom or equality, are linked to what we refer to as our ideals. Whereas the super-ego commands, prescribes and prohibits, threatening (internal) punishment in order to achieve obedience (the strictures of conscience), the ego ideal functions in a very different way. As Hanly (1984) notes, there is a crucial difference between the avoidance of dishonesty because one is anxious about the guilt one would feel if one transgressed the injunction to be honest, and the pursuit of honesty because one sees it as a positive virtue, that this is the kind of person one would like to be. The ego ideal therefore represents the ethical self as something to be achieved, and the inability to achieve leads to disappointment, shame and loss but not necessarily to guilt.

Our research once more suggests the powerful role of identificatory processes in the formation of the ego ideal and the establishment of values. However, it is clear that the identifications that foster the development of our ideals are not just concentrated in the early experiences of family life but are spread across the life course, perhaps particularly in the teenage and young adult period. Here is Don, a community worker, talking about some formative identifications in his own life. Don comes from a white working-class background. In our interviews with him he painted his father in rather grey colours whereas his mother, a seamstress, was much more vivid. Referring to his own values he said:

> 'I think I had a sort of socialist idea of things when, erm, it's not from my dad really, he was sort of middle of the road, it was from my mum was more, but my uncles really who lived up in Salford, and they were kind of heroes to me really....'

One of them he described thus:

> 'He was like a professional footballer in the '40s. He talked about the minimum wage and all those kinds of things and he was sort of into chess and he liked the Russian way of life and all this kind, quite a strict religious man ... but you know really kind of disciplined in his life. I liked that side of things....'

> '... I can remember once that it was when Mountbatten got blown up ... and I was talking to him and saying wasn't it bad and he said "no, not at all", he said, "it's a good thing". And I was really shocked that, you know, the fact that he was applauding a violent act and a violent act against the Royal family and we kind of got into a discussion about that, and it's kind of, I suppose, that was a kind of catalyst then, before that I hadn't really had any views either way.'

Later in the interview Don himself makes connections between his earlier life and his present beliefs about the voluntary and community sector:

> 'I like, you know, I like people to do a good day's work really, so I kind of got a bit of discipline, in that sense, 'cos of Stalinist uncles ... I'm not kind of laid back, "oh yeh, just do what you want".'

Don's uncles embodied an appealing mixture of rebelliousness, egalitarianism and discipline. Subsequently Don brought these values to the ways in which he manages other community workers and in particular the importance he attaches to evaluation, a methodology that has become particularly associated with the modernisation of governance, something Don otherwise had little time for:

> 'I think there's a lot of poor practice around ... there's a lot of people who are out for themselves within the, what I call "Poverty Industry" ... you know we should try and challenge some of that, that might seem as a kind of bureaucratic approach to things ... I think that's a good way to challenge some of the bad practice that goes on. So I've kind of got that as a sort of discipline as well as my worldview.'

We can see from this example how important Don's uncles were as a catalyst for the development of his own ideals in his teenage years. But there is a difference between identification and internalisation. Don admits himself that for a while he expressed his values in a quite arrogant and 'bolshie' way. There was a crude and indigested quality to them, a lack of reflexivity about them. It is as if his identification with his uncles was immediate and concrete, and he became a version (parody) of them.

Where values are built on unworked-through identifications we tend to over-identify with them. Such values are brittle rather than strong, and strident rather than firm. They need a moral landscape that is unambiguous, where there is no need for orientation because everything is clear. In contrast, values built on internalisation are fallible but crucial devices for finding our way around moral space. They provide orientation at the shifting and uncertain intersections of class, 'race', gender, culture, or institution. But it is only orientation, only a sense of 'this is the way we should go' as we stumble around in the dark.

Ideals without idealisation

The question is then, when does an ideal become idealised? Hanly (1984) examines this in terms of the subtle distinction between the ego ideal and the ideal ego, an idealising mirror that has a consolatory function for the self. In the realm of human values, therefore, the greatest danger is a moral narcissism in which virtue, and specifically the virtue one believes that one embodies and upholds, becomes fetishised. The resulting moralism expresses a superior attitude in which all virtue has been gathered in to one's own side. We can see here the traces of the splitting characteristic of Klein's paranoid–schizoid position. Eunice reflects on this moralism when she expresses her reservations about the time when, in her university years, she was a punk involved in direct action and living in a squat in London:

[Interviewer: 'What kind of reservations?']

'Just about how very dogmatic people were and how we saw the world in extremely black and white terms, and how harshly judgemental I was and how cliquey and kind of exclusive it could be, you know, in the name of all those nice values about social justice and equality and things like that, you actually set up new categories in which to judge and exclude people … it became another sort of fixed identity and a way of identifying the self against others all the time. And trying to think that in some way you were superior to other people even though your political work is supposedly all about equality and, you know, freedom and things.'

Interestingly, later Eunice adds, "you know, all those kind of values are still there, I just think I hold them differently". Returning to the dilemma she faced over the disciplining of her colleague we can say with confidence that it was because Eunice had strong values but held them differently that she faced a dilemma at all. For unless one resorts to moral narcissism (a position from which one can do no wrong), to have strong values these days means to feel the pull of the different claims corresponding to one's different identities. Eunice did what she thought was right and in making this judgement about rights and wrongs she acted ethically. According to Banks and Williams (2005), in resolving an ethical dilemma 'a choice is made, usually after much thought and agonizing, and one alternative is judged to be less bad/ unwelcome than the other. But because the choice still involves the violation of some moral principle or requirement, moral agents may nevertheless feel remorse or regret at the decision made or the action taken' (p 1012). Following Bernard Williams, Banks refers to this as the 'remainder'.

Eunice clearly experienced 'the remainder'. Speaking of her colleague she said:

> 'He resigned in the end ... but it was not a good ending, you know, it was quite a bad ending and I did try and get him to come in to have a sort of [...] and talk over, but he didn't come, so it's kind, that's kind of been left hanging.'

Later she added:

> '... at the end of it I just, I would've liked to have been able to talk to him and hope to get him to see that he was misunderstanding parts of the process and that, that it was actually fair, and as per the policy but he didn't turn up to us, the meeting that we arranged.'

There is a clear sense of regret in these statements, a sense of things finishing in an unsatisfactory way, with hurt feelings on both sides and then an attempt to make it all better and put right a situation, an attempt which did not succeed. This is immediately followed by another statement that expresses the realisation that things sometimes cannot be put right:

> 'You can't always persuade them to change their minds, so sometimes you just have to accept there will be people out there who will have whatever reason to gripe about what we do or feel slighted or, and you have to let them get on with it.'

The discomfort Eunice felt about the way things were left 'hanging' is in addition to the discomfort she felt as she was going through the process. The former is the 'remainder' and the components of it are complex. First, there is a reparative desire to make things better, to repair the situation. Linked to this one senses that there is also anxiety about the possibility of retaliatory attack if things are not resolved (that is, her anxiety that the black community would side with her colleague against her). There is also, as she put it, "my tendency to be a bit of a control freak and wanna make sure everything is completely right all the time ... that ability to let go and accept things as they are rather than trying to fix everything". Here Eunice expresses both the desire for omnipotent control and, through Zen (something that she practised), the acceptance of its impossibility. Finally, and this is different to the desire for reparation, there is the need to be loved, "change his mind and have him love us and think we were great".

So what can we conclude from Eunice's example? First, that one can be caught in a dilemma and yet still be clear about what it is that one has to do. Second, 'resolving' a dilemma rarely refers to a single decision but to a course of action that may stretch out over months (or, presumably, years). Third, in pursuing this course of action the ethical agent is persecuted by doubts that relate both to potential weaknesses and faults both in themselves and in the chosen course of action (the bad within the good) and to the potential value in the course of action rejected (the good within the bad). Fourth, once the action is completed there remains a complex remainder of feelings that are clearly influenced by the personality of the actor.

We can see how ethical action is saturated with feeling and yet despite these powerful affects Eunice finds a course through the painful uncertainty of it all. Eunice acts in what we have called the 'depressive' or 'tragic' position, a position in which conflicting internal feelings can be held without splitting them and projecting them onto others and therefore a position from which the complexity of social relations can be fully grasped. The world is not black and white; the illusion of the moral narcissist, of always 'being in the right', is rejected. The tragic dimension of social relations is apprehended but while this depressive attitude is characterised by doubt and regret it should not be confused with depression. Eunice remains strong. She has a belief in herself and her capacity to make good decisions in spite of her doubts. In this sense she embodies an ordinary hopefulness, a hopefulness that, in Samuel Beckett's famous phrase, enables her to 'fail better'.

Beck (1997) provides a celebration of doubt as something befitting the ethics of a radically modern identity. As he puts it, 'when it is doubtful whether one is right or in the possession of the truth, when the questions lie in that area where correctness and falsity overlap, when self-doubts chew up the arrogance, then enemies are no longer enemies, nor are they brothers with whom one dances in festivals of solidarity; instead, they are fellow or opposing doubters' (p 169). Yet

Beck seems unable to appreciate that doubt alone disarms us. Assailed by doubt Eunice is nevertheless able to steer a course and she is able to do this because her values provide her with the guidance she needs and her sense of her own authority provides her with the confidence to risk finding her way. We live in an increasingly plural world and yet also one in which both state and corporate power become ever more concentrated. In such a world the capacity for ethical agency is vital. Yes, we must doubt, but we must also act.

In summary, our argument is that if the development worker is to rise to the challenges posed by globalisation and modernisation there are at least three different kinds of internal resource they need to be able to draw on. First, they need the psychological capacity (the capacity to stay in the tragic position) to face the increasing moral complexity of their working environment. Second, they need a sense of their own authority without which the complexity of different views and claims that surround them will reduce them to a state of agonised indecision. Third, they need a firm set of values, held in a non-idealised way, which can provide orientation in dilemmatic space.

SEVEN

Handling authority relations

Power and authority relations pervade development work

Development workers are immersed in complex relations of power and authority, two related although too often blurred concepts. Authority is central to the analysis of public institutions and needs to be explored as such, together with an exploration of the underlying structures of power that underpin them. Development workers are centrally involved with the impact of decisions made by those with power and authority, as these decisions impact on the communities that they serve: policy decisions with significant implications for public services such as housing, education, health and welfare provision, for example. The development worker has a brief to enable service users and communities to challenge such decisions, unpacking the structures of power that underpin them and calling authorities to account as part of the democratic process. But this is only one dimension of authority, as this impacts on the development role. Authority not only attaches to formal positions within state bureaucracies but is also crucial to the exercise of discretion by public officials, particularly in negotiating the dilemmas of face-to-face 'street-level' work (Lipsky, 1980). Development workers exercise authority themselves, whether positively or negatively, when facilitating or containing the frustrations and conflicts within communities. In such a 'dilemmatic space' where values, meanings and actions, means and ends, are highly contested, the effective use of one's own authority is critical in relation to both axes of power and authority.

In this chapter we re-examine a number of existing analyses of power and authority in the light of our research. First we identify how some of the dilemmas of regeneration work involve the exercise, negotiation or contestation of authority. We then examine earlier attempts to theorise power and authority, from Max Weber through to Richard Sennett, using our research to illustrate these approaches before offering some criticisms and alternatives. We suggest that alternative approaches need to offer a more dynamic model of authority relations, less institutionally oriented, giving less emphasis to 'positional authority' and additional consideration to 'reputational' and/or 'personal' authority. We argue that the latter is particularly pertinent to the exercise of discretion and we offer an examination of its origins and the ways in which it is mediated by considerations of class, 'race' and gender. For the development worker to have a 'good-enough' inner authority to cope with the competing pressures and demands of their role requires an exploratory journey through one's own relations of authority. We conclude by illustrating the importance of a critical awareness of self, as well as a critical awareness of the structural relations of power and public authority.

Paradoxes of the development role

Development work raises questions about the use of authority, as well as raising questions about how to respond to the authority of powerful others, questions made more complex by the ways in which the asymmetries of power inherent in the professional/non-professional relationship are overlain by other asymmetries such as black/white, local/outsider, working class/middle class, female/male. Nor is the exercise of authority necessarily made any easier by resort to terms such as the 'primary task' or the 'operational objectives' – terms used to identify professional priorities in public service provision. In development work, there are so often competing agendas and conflicting definitions of purpose, including underlying conflicts of interest between public policy priorities and professional goals and values. As one youth worker put this:

> 'I came into this work because I wanted to help young people with their problems, not because I thought, like our government now does, that young people are a problem.'

Another respondent, a senior manager in a local youth service, makes a similar point:

> 'What I'm expected to deliver ... is based on the government initiative around reducing crime or targeting young people who are seen to be deficient ... and I don't believe that ... for those young people, their life chances are so blighted and they feel so damaged, then it's my generation and the generation before me that caused that damage and for ... anyone to blame those young people ... is palpably wrong.... There's no justice in that....'

Such responsibilities place development professionals right on the boundaries between state and civil society; their task is to facilitate the strengthening of civil society, building and supporting community and voluntary organisations, enabling citizens to better engage in public life even when such work involves conflict with the state and its agendas. Paradoxically, the very act of questioning authority and suggesting that alternative approaches may be possible can define the development worker as an 'authority' in the eyes of those at the receiving end of public policy interventions. Whether explicitly or implicitly, strengthening civil society involves struggles in relation to authority – just as such struggles can themselves strengthen the reputational authority of the development worker with his/her community of service users. S/he can become defined as the authoritative expert, however strenuously s/he strives to play a facilitating rather than a leading role.

Development work involves questioning and challenging particular models and practices of authority such as many of those that characterise the paternalistic state, the impervious and non-responsive state or the neglectful or over-intrusive state. Development work also offers opportunities to explore and to experiment with alternative models of authority through self-organisation and collective action. One of the key challenges here is to develop alternatives that do not even unwittingly reproduce the very relations of authority that had been the subject of criticism in the first place, throwing up new hierarchies with structures of power and authority that may be no less oppressive for being less explicit or transparent (the 'tyranny of structurelessness', as second wave feminists described these types of non-collective collectives).

The role of the development worker can be characterised, then, as being both, 'in and against authority'. They are in positions of authority in the sense that they have some (if limited) authority over resources and some potential scope for providing positive models of authority, acting as mentors and guides, while enabling others to take up their own authority, constructively. A worker's consistent 'effective' exercise of authority can influence people's sense of themselves as individuals and communities with capacities, as well as rights.

Development workers who speak and act with authority can also trigger more negative responses, by arousing feelings of intimidation and resentment. While using their authority to gain access to resources, to establish and negotiate legitimacy and credibility, and to demonstrate ways of navigating public authority systems without losing sight of the underlying structures of power and interests involved, the development role requires practitioners to remain sensitive to such negative feelings,

feelings that can produce increasing alienation, rather than increasing user and community empowerment. There are difficult balancing acts to be managed here. Even some of the most experienced practitioners find difficulties in striking such a balance, remaining critically aware of the need to challenge hierarchical structures of power and authority constructively while simultaneously expressing their own authority as development professionals. One participant expressed her unease thus:

> 'I don't like hierarchies, so I've never liked working for anyone else ... so I find it difficult when I am actually part of a hierarchy ... if I have to chair something and I have to assume some kind of authority which also means I have to deal with problems. I really like working collaboratively.'

Practitioners can feel additionally ambivalent about calling on the legitimacy of their professional expertise given the deep vein of anti-professionalism that pervades the occupational histories of development work. Citizens of disadvantaged communities are just as likely to perceive the state's professional representatives as sources of their troubles and may hesitate before trusting those tasked with community development.

Public professionals can also experience tensions between their professional roles and their status as employees. Accepting or voicing challenges, being transparent or questioning one's own authority and that of others may all be appropriate within welfare practice, for example, but may be considered fundamentally inappropriate within a managerialist frame of reference. Such tensions can be most sharply felt by those middle managers who are both practising professionals but also managing others, with accountability upwards to senior management. Located on the insecure boundaries of their organisation, these development workers need regular reaffirmation of their authority. But if they challenge organisational policies they risk having their own authority undermined by more senior managers and politicians.

Within the context of declining levels of many public services, anxieties over the potential decline of social capital and diminishing public interest in formal politics, greater importance has been accorded to the value of relational skills in development work. Emphasis has been placed on public participation, user involvement, partnership working, volunteering and capacity building to promote user and community engagement in structures of governance (Newman, 2001; Miller, 2004). However, the state has also attempted to micro-manage the relational and indeterminate aspects of the development role, thereby exacerbating its inherent tensions.

Power and authority

According to classical pluralist analyses of power, for individuals or social groups to exercise power is to bring about outcomes, making things happen, getting others to do things even when it is against their wishes or interests and despite any resistance on their part (Dahl, 1961). Power operates on three inter-connected levels: the interpersonal, organisational and societal. The possession of unequally distributed, scarce and desirable resources provides the basis of power over others, along with a willingness and capacity to exercise that advantage in part by anticipating the wants of others and their capacity to resist (French and Raven, 1959). In his critique of this pluralist position Lukes (1974) argued that the exercise of power over others does not need to be explicit or intentional but can be hidden, tacit and institutionalised. So deep-seated are the rules and structures, people may not realise when they are acting against their own interests, thereby removing the need for the powerful to exercise their power in concerted ways. Here Lukes draws on Gramsci's notion of hegemony (1974), the way in which subaltern groups consent to their own domination because of the ruling classes' monopoly of the means of persuasion and legitimation. However, to the extent that everyone attempts to utilise the resources that are available to them in order to bring about some outcome or to resist the power of others, all are power-exercising beings. Michel Foucault (1977, 1980) argued that power is a central feature of social life, circulating through the whole social body and saturating every relationship. Others have argued the underlying importance of the power to control and use the economic resources essential for survival, resources that have been perceived as fundamental in shaping the organisation of social life.

Explorations of power that draw on Marxist analyses emphasise precisely this. They point to the significance of underlying relationships of economic power within capitalist societies, relations that underpin class inequalities, setting the frameworks within which political power is to be exercised and legitimated. From these perspectives, the current predominance of neoliberalism illustrates precisely this – with public policies framed in ways that tend to re-enforce, rather than fundamentally challenge, market interests. Paulo Freire drew on Marxist analyses of power and legitimacy, as these had been developed by Gramsci, recognising the significance of Gramsci's influence in his later writings (Freire, 1995): 'I discovered that I had been greatly influenced by Gramsci', he commented, 'long before I had read him' (p 64). Like Gramsci, Freire emphasised the importance of challenging dominant 'common-sense' (hegemonic) ideas, if the oppressed are to develop critical consciousness, reflecting and acting on their world, in order to change it (Freire, 1972).

John Gaventa's more recent approach to the analysis of power has provided additional tools of particular relevance for development workers internationally as well as more locally (Gaventa, 2006). His 'power cube' provides a three-dimensional model, including Lukes' distinctions between explicit, implicit and hidden forms of power, along with two further dimensions. The space dimension distinguishes between 'closed', 'invited' and 'claimed' spaces of power, identifying whether spaces are 'closed' to communities, whether communities are 'invited' into spaces (that is, invited to join in consultation exercises in order to participate on decision makers' terms) or whether spaces have been 'claimed' – spaces that have been opened up as a result of collective action. Finally, the power cube's third dimension distinguishes whether power is being exercised locally, nationally or internationally (increasing evidently in the context of increasing globalisation). Taken together, this power cube offers an innovative tool for developing a critical understanding of underlying power structures, providing the basis for developing more effective strategies for progressive social change.

With some exceptions (Sennett, 1980; Raz, 1979, 1990) fewer attempts have been made to develop and apply the concept of authority since Max Weber's (1968) classical study. Both political science and sociology have focused more extensively on power rather than authority, while organisational studies have been more preoccupied with analysing leadership. Authority has been more central to the Group Relations tradition where it has been developed in a specific way to refer to personal, role-based authority (Miller, 1993).

To be in a position of authority, like a surgeon or airline pilot, has typically been considered as a form of legitimate power and subsumed within this. Weber's classic work identified legitimate authority as resting on one of three systems of social control. According to Weber, those with power are accorded authority because of the legitimacy of the principles by which they hold this power. Authority can be based on tradition (as in the case of hereditary monarchies, for example). Alternatively, authority can be based on charisma (as in the case of populist leaders). And finally, a legal-rational authority is one that is underpinned by formal rules and professional/bureaucratic expertise (more typically the case, in principle at least, within Western democracies).

Carter (1979) suggests that pure authority is the antithesis of force (p 17). It implies the capacity to command respect and elicit voluntary compliance in the form of unhesitating obedience or considered acceptance (Carter, 1979, p 22), or what could be better described as 'followership'. Without this a surgeon or airline pilot could not do their job. Alternatively, for Raz authority is defined as normative power, consisting of the ability to change pre-existing norms and patterns of action ('protected reasons') by providing alternative and 'overriding' reasons for action (Raz, 1979, p 18). Effective authority is feasible, according to this view, only when it is regarded by a sufficient number of people as legitimate. From each of these perspectives then, authority involves a specific form of power, the power to provide leadership with legitimacy.

With the exception of Weber's concept of charismatic authority a core assumption has been that authority belongs primarily to a formally sanctioned role. The legitimacy of such positional authority depends on the recognition given by those who are subject to it. Yet it also depends on the occupant's capacity and motivation to perform the role in question. It has been acknowledged that if a succession of incumbents perform a given role incompetently or inappropriately then this might ultimately undermine the legitimacy of the role itself. Elected politicians, for example, can undermine the role of the democratic representative in regimes that are particularly corrupt or inefficient. But this has not been a major focus of research. Indeed, authority has been treated in a rather undynamic way, as if it were something stable and fixed. Much less attention has been given to exploring the efforts required of an individual role holder to secure and retain legitimacy, or to how legitimacy can be lost, or how new voices of authority are created, often in defiance of existing ones (Lovell, 2003). For example, someone may use their personal authority to defy an acknowledged authority, applying considerable effort and skill in a calculated attempt to displace, challenge or de-legitimise it (Carter, 1979). Thus authority is relational: the nature of compliance is critical. Carter's insight on this has been extremely useful although it has remained relatively under-developed. There are important implications here for the role of the development worker, balancing different authority relations, in continuing processes of challenge and change.

For Friedman (1973), mutual recognition between the holder and the subject of authority is the most essential aspect of its legitimacy – the 'shared recognition of entitlement' (Lukes, 1987, p 209). Lukes (1987) highlights a number of problems with this approach, pointing to the more complex reality of diversity, competition and conflict. He notes that mutual recognition is not always necessary to sustain authority. Nor is the recognition of those 'in authority' or those recognised as 'an authority' necessarily based on culturally shared beliefs and values, as Flathman has suggested (Flathman, 1990). According to Lukes, relations of authority are complex, involving processes of interpretation and different perspectives, including the perspectives of the holder of authority, the perspectives of those subject to this authority and those observing it. This offers a more multilayered view of authority, a view of authority as inherently unstable, subject to conflict, negotiation, renegotiation and change – a more layered view that would seem more relevant for an understanding of the complexities that development workers need to address.

One such aspect of this complexity involves the distinction between someone who is 'in authority', someone who 'is an authority' (and therefore commands a respectful hearing), and a person who has what might be thought of as an 'inner authority', the authority that is embodied or expressed in his or her person. These three different forms of authority refer to position, reputation and the self, respectively. Although each is distinct, in practice each can have a relationship to the others. For example, someone who is *an authority* could be expected to also be *in authority*. But once we get beyond institutions to civil society we can see that this may not always be the case. In the groups, networks and associations of civil society people are often recognised as an authority because of their local reputation even though they may have no formal (positional) authority. Local 'wise women' often operated in this way, as do 'elders' in many migrant communities.

Within the psychodynamic tradition authority has been thought of primarily in its institutional settings but has nevertheless been given a very specific meaning:

> I conceptualise "personal authority" as a function of managing oneself in relation to role and task performance, while 'power' is concerned with maintenance and enhancement of status and with control over other people. (Miller, 1993, p 310)

From this perspective, authority does not imply 'commitment to the prevailing power structure or to the established way of doing things' (Miller, 1993, p 311). Rather, authority is derived from personal competence to the task of the organisation. Its exercise can involve personal risk to the individual concerned, however. This tradition sees the organisation's task as constantly prone to becoming undermined (Chapman, 2003), from collusive patterns of behaviour involving both those in positions of authority and their subordinates. This approach focuses on the paradox that managers and managed can become trapped in a dependent relationship to the status quo. As Miller puts it, 'the work organisation is maintained as a hierarchy of dependency and compliance' (Miller, 1993, p 292). This tradition's weakness is its unproblematic way of thinking about an organisation's primary task (Silverman, 1968). Thus Carr (2001) argues that 'authority is an aspect of a person's role and that may only be discovered in relation to task' (Carr, 2001, p 55). In the public sphere, however, concepts of task and purpose are always and necessarily contested (Hoggett, 2005a). This is particularly the case for development professionals, located as they tend to be on organisational boundaries, in and between civil society and the state. Like the notion of authority itself, the public sphere and public services are constantly subject to contestation, negotiation, re-negotiation and challenge.

Limitations of orthodox concepts of authority

The concentration on research on positional authority has led to some neglect of the workings of authority within civil society. Here informal roles predominate and the part played by the individual, both in establishing and retaining a reputation, is of critical importance. Considerable effort is required to maintain relationships and to be seen to be doing the right thing in order to sustain any authority accorded. Traditional institutionalised approaches need to acknowledge the importance of such horizontal relations of authority in social networks and small groups.

Although located within contexts marked by structural inequalities of power, relations of authority cannot simply be reduced to these. Underlying power structures may not be so evident in specific contexts, such as multiagency/professional partnerships where there are no formal single decision-making roles, for example. Similarly, specific roles can have a loose relationship to wider organisational structures, allowing for the exercise of considerable discretion and autonomy. This situation has been identified with the very nature of the development worker's boundary role, one that is simultaneously both 'inside' and 'outside' the organisation.

Approaches to authority that focus on static rather than dynamically unfolding relationships also have limitations, failing to account for the functioning of authority within a range of relationships such as those between parent and child, teacher and pupil, supervisor and trainee, development worker and citizen/community group – relationships in which authority may be deliberately transitional. The goal of development may be defined as constituting precisely this – that there should come a point in time when those with authority will no longer command it. Development workers should no longer have the need to do so, as citizens and communities exercise their own authority. In such situations the responsibility of those in authority is to facilitate exactly such a shift in the balance of the relationship, so that the other can become autonomous, valuing their own sense of authority and acting on it. In other words, the exercise of authority is itself an authorising process. One participant in our study captured this neatly, pointing out that:

> '… authority should allow young people to grow rather than impose.'

As another respondent reflected, to achieve a relationship of mutual respect involves recognising that young people have problems while rejecting the idea that they *are* a problem. With appropriate support (from a 'good authority') in his view, young people can find their own authority for themselves.

Where authority is transitional, by definition, its expression will change over time. Initially, a professional may assume considerable knowledge of the needs of the other and may act on this. As the relationship evolves s/he may offer advice rather than 'instruct', acting as a reflective listener, offering confirmatory responses to strategies devised by the other. Investment in a sustainable relationship of authority, albeit one that is changing and contains the seeds of its own dissolution, requires that it is open to challenge and is transparent. The boundaries of authority need to be negotiated and re-negotiated to achieve agreed understandings.

Internalised authority

Good authority is hard to find and disappointments are all too frequent. As one participant remarked, reflecting on one such disappointment:

> 'I've never been so annoyed about anything … I try to establish a certain kind of relationship with senior people … based on us being adults, about being able to say things to

each other that we need to say … allowing the possibilities
of dialogue … that's all been rubbished.'

Freud highlighted the fundamental importance of an internalised
authority and its origins in the family. Freud argued that the child exists
initially in a state of total dependence on its parents, its first and foremost
authority figures. Unlike later object-relational psychoanalysis Freud
highlighted the role of the father, a patriarchal stance subsequently
challenged by psychoanalytic feminists such as Benjamin (1978).
Despite such differences, psychoanalysts agree that early experiences
leave traces that continue to surface in adult life and interact with
subsequent experiences of authority in the school, the neighbourhood,
the workplace and elsewhere. Thus how we react to or take up our
own authority tends to be at least to some extent related to our
previous experiences (although we may not always be conscious of
these connections). For example, Gus spoke warmly of his childhood
in the surroundings of a miner's terraced house:

'… it was very secure, very warm, very – quite strict in
places but very warm upbringing and I can only look back
with … remember it with pleasure.'

Although Gus felt he was a disappointment to his parents having not
pursued his formal education further, he also felt supported:

'… my father was quite adamant that he did not, he did not
expect or want me ever to go near a coal mine. Therefore
achieving academic … was very important and I did achieve
that … but I got out of school when I was fifteen and a
half … my father and my mother although they were …
disappointed, they were able to say, "Well, what do you want?
How can we, you know, how can we support you to go on?"
… my father understood much more that actually I had a
very strong belief system, in justice and right or wrong …
when I got involved in political activities, trade unionism
… in strikes and whatever, he understood that. So, he did
recognise that actually I was achieving.'

These positive supporting relationships have, in his view, influenced
how he relates to young people, in his turn, focusing on enabling them
to find their own goals for themselves.

Those who have had difficult relationships with key authority figures, such as parents or care givers, in which core needs have been denied, may well continue to struggle to find either their own authoritative voice or to engage effectively with other authority figures. This is not necessarily the case, however. Take, for example, one of our female respondents, Bella. She was in her mid-thirties and grew up in an unskilled working-class family with working parents who later separated. Although she was very fond of her mother, appreciative of the difficulties she had faced, and glad that she was now in a satisfying relationship, Bella did not see her mother as a role model. Bella's father was an alcoholic authoritarian man, which led to domestic violence. He had low self-esteem and was both deferential and hostile towards authority. He believed that his daughters should not attempt to "get above their station" and he refused to allow them to continue at school beyond the minimum leaving age. Bella's insistence on returning to education after one brief unsatisfying experience of working life combined with constant conflict over her father's drinking and resulted in her father throwing her out of the family home.

On discovering development work, largely by accident, Bella remains working in her home neighbourhood and is at her most creative and energetic when working with young people. It is perhaps significant that unlike many of her middle-class professional colleagues she has no romantic attachment to the neighbourhood or any desire to keep young people in this area when they grow up. From her own experience she knows that there is a world to be explored and what young people need primarily are the tools and information to enable them to take authority for themselves.

Surviving abusive authority

For some, there is the more demanding challenge of addressing the experience of damaging and abusive forms of authority where trust has been broken. Abuse, arising from those relationships in which we are at our most vulnerable, is that which breaches, invades or violates our personal physical or emotional selves, our bodily integrity (Williams, 1999). Beyond such abuse of authority lies an authoritarianism that shows no respect and denies our autonomy and humanity.

Gina is a middle-aged black woman who, after many years of unpaid activism, worked as a neighbourhood manager in the city where she lived. Her struggle to develop a sense of her own authority was acute. Abandoned by her mixed race mother, whom she described as suffering from paranoid schizophrenia, she never met her father and spent the first 21 years of her life in the care system. For the first 15 years she was brought up in an affluent white middle-class environment but this had a damaging impact. She left to go to London where, in other care homes, she was subjected to various forms of abuse, and had an abortion when she was 16. After a brief spell in prison she became a single parent at 19. After her second child was born she was caught up for a long period in a violent relationship with the child's father – "I just disappeared for a while", she reflected about this period in her life. She lived with her children on a white, racist estate where being pelted with stones on the way to school was a regular experience.

Gina survived, she explained, mainly because of the support she received from particular individuals. These included the two midwives who delivered her first child and then took her home with them and cared for her and the baby for over six months and the housing officer who helped to re-house her, secured an injunction against a violent partner, provided her with encouragement sense and confidence, and pointed her in the direction of a career. These professionals offered Gina a model of 'good authority' that enabled her to retain some faith in adults and regain some trust that not all authority was abusive:

> 'All through my life it's been about surviving really', she reflected, 'it's been about finding the skills to survive in the world … and I think that's the drive I've got inside me…. It's really the people along the way that I've met, that I've made friends with and they're like a network. They are my family….'

Developing a 'good-enough' sense of authority

The first part of Richard Sennett's book *Authority* (1980) is an exploration of the impasse between bad authority and resistance to it. Resistance is understood as the recourse of the weak – children, oppressed workers – and Sennett concentrates on its limitations, 'the weak could resist only by being the negative of whatever the powerful wanted them to be' (1980, p 72). Through a series of case studies, from psychotherapy, industrial relations and literature, Sennett examines forms of false authority and false resistance.

One of the key forms of false resistance is that of 'disobedient dependence', with its archetype the adolescent rebellion. Sennett notes how this kind of resistance leads to forms of conflict that actually bind the antagonists together, 'the very act of disobeying, with all its confrontations, anxieties, and conflicts, knits people together' (Sennett,

1980, p 33). To suggest that this is 'rebelling against authority is a mistake', rather it is 'rebelling "within" authority' (1980, p 33). Sennett suggests that too often our rejection of authority is not accompanied by an alternative vision or a better version: we are unable to create after we have negated. Jean-Jacques Rousseau ([1755]/1993) expressed a similar idea, 'peoples once accustomed to masters are not in a condition to do without them' (pp 33-4). The Brazilian educator, Paulo Freire, whose work has been seminal in development practice, as well as inspiring adult educators worldwide, echoes this view. Freire focused on developing through popular education a critical consciousness to transform social relations rather than to replace one set of oppressors by another (Freire, 1973).

The need for authority, and the resultant dependency, conflicts with another equally powerful need, that of individual freedom. This can partially explain the existence of a strong antipathy towards or fear of authority, a fear often reinforced by the behaviour of those 'in authority'. No doubt our reaction to authority is also deeply entangled in our ambivalence about being recognised as an authority ourselves. For Sennett, a good authority symbolises strength, solidity and stability over time. It is precisely someone 'who will use his strength to care for others' (Sennett, 1980, p 82).

> Authority is ... a matter of defining and interpreting differences in strength ... the sentiment of authority is the recognition just that these differences exist ... it is a matter of taking account of the needs and desires of the weak as well as of the strong once these differences have been acknowledged. (Sennett, 1980, p 126)

If, as Sennett argues, authority can be thought of as representing strength and containment, then the 'good authority' acts as a safe harbour. This offers shelter from the storms of growing independence and a place of return for purposes of recuperation, reflection and re-learning. Good authority needs to be able to contain the hopes, fears and fantasies, confused and contradictory perceptions and experiences about authority itself. What now remains for the transformed active subject is respect and appreciation for the work undertaken by the mentor or guide, fulfilling the obligations of the mentoring role through the exercise of such authority. The following describes one individual's journey from 'rebelling within authority' to an emerging sense of personal authority, the fragility of which is revealed when the individual finds himself having to engage with senior management. It is then that the vulnerabilities associated with his class background reappear.

We explored some of the identifications that contributed to Don's values in the previous chapter. Don grew up on a housing estate in a major city. As a teenager he skirted with trouble, had an "attitude problem", as he put it, left school without much in the way of qualifications, worked in a paint factory until the age of 27 and then got into youth work after the sudden death of his much loved younger brother. He has been an active trade unionist even after he moved into his present local authority management position. Don seems at ease with taking up his own authority in relation to those with whom he is working. He welcomes a structured approach with voluntary and community organisations. He is cynical about much of what he refers to as "the poverty industry", and believes strongly in challenging bad practice. He is confident about his ability to work effectively in situations that are highly charged or politically sensitive and is not afraid to intervene, as the following extract of an interview indicates:

> [Interviewer: 'Were you kind of comfortable with the authority you carried into that situation?']

> 'Yeah I am actually. It's interesting, I am, 'cos I, it's because I believe that, I believe that it needs to change. I really believe that ... [and] I think local residents, I think the membership, they wanna see change. So I felt it is a kind of just cause really and I know there are one or two really ... dodgy bad people out there.... So yeah, but I've got no problem with that authority. But I don't think I come across as authoritarian ... I come across as ... I'm leading it.'

We examined the importance of Don's two chess-playing, footballer and communist uncles in an earlier chapter. Don attaches much importance to telling things exactly as they are, as straight as he can. He has deployed this to good effect, acquiring a reputation as someone who can be trusted. He also is aware of how this differs from his early professional years when he would just 'dive in' to situations without thinking.

Don had little respect for his immediate boss but this rejection helped shape his own idea of authority and he found in a woman colleague someone to admire and to be copied. Don relished the dilemmas and conflicts of the job:

> '... the fact that there are ... dilemmas, conflicts and tensions
> – I think that's kind of, makes the job interesting.'

So, whereas the area where he worked, involving allegations of corruption in black-led community organisations, had become a virtual 'no go' area for most professionals, Don enjoyed the challenge of working effectively there:

> 'I kinda like the chess thing – it's like a bit of a chess game really.'

While Don is comfortable with his authority he cannot identify with management and sees management meetings as largely a waste of time. He talked at length about his own lack of confidence and his tendency to avoid senior management so that he belonged neither to his workforce peer group nor to the circle of his immediate managers. He also noted how this paralleled the difficulties of growing up on a working-class estate and of managing relations with the tougher children at the school. He acknowledged how both the recognition of what he had achieved and the departure of a co-manager, who was both confident and authoritative in her work, had brought him out of the shadows and left him with far greater confidence. He now had to find an authoritative voice in those managerial spaces he had previously left to his former co-manager, but he had space to breathe and felt sufficiently recognised that he could signal his ambition to take on more senior roles.

In search of good authority

As we saw earlier, at the heart of Sennett's analysis is the concept of 'recognition', a concept central to Hegelian thought, to contemporary political theory (Honneth, 1995) and psychoanalysis (Benjamin, 1990, 2004). In summary, from this perspective good authority is that which promotes mutual recognition. By this Sennett means the recognition of the independent existence of the other and her/his needs and experiences, where recognition has elements of both acceptance and valuation. While the need for acceptance and recognition emerge as powerful themes, however, our research also provides evidence of more transformative demands.

Sennett and Benjamin envisage a struggle towards a form of mutual recognition in which asymmetries of authority and dependency will continue but in a relationship where each party now feels respected.

With each shift in the consciousness of self and other there comes a change in behaviour towards others and in turn this change produces a change in the other's behaviour. In other words, we can act cooperatively if we play neither the victim nor the master, or in Benjamin's (2004) terms, neither the 'done to' nor the 'doer'. Development promises to promote precisely such changes, to promote a critical consciousness in Freire's terminology towards individual and community empowerment, enabling young people and adults to develop different kinds of relationships with authority, struggling for more equal relationships, in the context of longer-term agendas for social justice, agendas that move on to challenge the underlying structures of inequality in capitalist societies.

Marx criticised Hegel for his idealism in which 'mind' or 'self-consciousness' was the essence of humankind and, 'religion, state power ... are spiritual entities' (Marx, 1970, p 176). Freedom for Hegel was a state of mind but the actual material relationships between people did not alter. In contrast, for Marx, human history, far from being an abstract process of the mind, was the struggle of real people in organised relations to each other, part of long-term processes of social change. Sennett suggests that in terms of a political programme of action two demands follow: that public authorities must be 'visible' and 'legible':

> Visible means that those who are in positions of control be explicit about themselves: clear about what they can and cannot do; explicit about their promises. 'Legible' specifies how this open statement can come about. (1980, p 168)

As participants in one of our group discussions noted, it was essential to be realistic and also to be transparent. "It's no good asking people what they want if you don't have the resources to meet the needs", commented one participant "– so don't get into that situation". Another added, "Never make promises that you can't keep", and admit it, openly, when mistakes have been made. Based on what Sennett describes as, 'the right and power to revise through discussion decisions which come from higher up' (1980, p 190), citizens must themselves through periodic disruptions to the chain of command, 'read', understand, collectively discuss, judge and revise the actions of authority. In this way, authority becomes a process, 'a making, breaking, remaking of meanings' (1980, p 190). Good practice is therefore dialogic, something ably demonstrated by Si in terms of the way in which he ran the youth club he was responsible for. Si insisted that all staff and volunteers should discuss all major issues and incidents.

He gave us an example: should they close the centre if there was a major incident? His staff wanted him to impose a strict line but he insisted that they had to think it through, "I've said each time there is a process that you go through and then you take the decision". In this particular case two young people stole a staff member's car from outside the centre; nevertheless our respondent opposed calls to close the centre the following night as this was an unfair form of 'blanket punishment'. He continued:

> 'Then people said they were feeling stressed, but I feel, professionally, you have to say, I'm upset because my colleague's car has got stolen, but actually I'm here to do this job and people have found that ... I think they've found that a bit stubborn.... So then there was an argument that young people need to know consequences. I said, yes, but the right people have got to know the consequences, not the wrong people. Um, and there's been quite a fierce argument and we're going to have to have, we will have a staff meeting about this.'

He provided another detailed example of someone he 'stood by', a man with a troubled past from the estate who had become a youth worker at the centre but who had failed to declare a number of crimes that he had committed since he had been employed with them. Si had taken risks in employing this man in the first place given the way in which contemporary public management is so risk-averse and he felt betrayed by him. Yet Si also realised that giving him the sack "would just be devastating for him" so he fought for an alternative course, involving a disciplinary and other measures, which his superiors reluctantly agreed to. One of the other measures was to ask the man to explain what he had done and to apologise for it at a full staff meeting. Perhaps unsurprisingly, even though Si saved the man's job, the man hated him for what he had had to do. Si's insistence that all important issues, including errors and failings, should be discussed openly, won him the respect, if not always the love, of his colleagues.

We believe that this commitment to an approach to one's own and others' authority which is transparent and contestable is founded on a basic hopefulness towards self and other, that we might, through interaction, become more than we are, and therefore on a belief in the potential for progressive social change, and a critical awareness of both social context and self. It is this approach that enables the development worker to bring authority to the role. Without it the individual is reduced to surface acting and impression management to cope with the demands of the job. Our research highlights the importance of personal authority, and the continuing struggle to secure and maintain this, if development professionals are to challenge effectively the misuse of authority in self and others.

Part Two
Modernisation and beyond

EIGHT

Modernisation and community governance

Modernisation has been a key theme for all three Labour administrations in Britain since 1997, with public service reform a central plank. As the Prime Minister's Strategy Unit pointed out in 2007, this was not simply a feature of the previous decade, either. The reform of public services had been a feature of previous governments since the Thatcher/ Major years of the last decades of the 20th century, as the state's role began to be reduced. Public service reform, the Strategy Unit argued, was now 'centred around the citizen consumer', with greater choice for service users, whether services were to be delivered by the state, the third sector, the private sector or some combination working in partnership together. Rather than acting as direct provider, then, the role of the state has become increasingly that of commissioner, enabler and performance manager, setting priorities. Labour administrations have particularly emphasised their role in target setting, aiming to bridge the gap between the quality of service provision in the most disadvantaged neighbourhoods compared with the national average, part of a national strategy to combat social exclusion. The government is 'flexible about who delivers services – public, private or third sector', focusing on ends not means, balancing top-down performance management and control with increasing choice for users shaping the service from below (Prime Minister's Strategy Unit, 2007).

This chapter sets out to unpack the assumptions underlying these policy statements, together with their varying implications for professional practice. To what extent do these policies differ from those of previous governments in the last two decades of the 20th century? How far are these policies internally consistent? Or have governments been trying to combine mutually conflicting policy objectives, striving to modernise public services through the increasing use of market mechanisms while simultaneously setting out to tackle poverty and social exclusion? And how have these differing policy initiatives impacted on front-line professionals working to promote participation in governance, active citizenship and empowerment among service users and among young people, particularly those living within disadvantaged neighbourhoods, identified as being in need of some form of professional intervention, professional modernisers who are, themselves, being professionally modernised?

While the focus of this chapter on modernisation and community governance is concentrated on the British context, British experiences do also need to be set within a wider framework. Far from representing a unique case, Britain's modernisation strategies have resonances with strategies to promote community engagement and empowerment internationally, strategies that had already been recognised as inherently problematic back in the 1990s, described as representing the human face of neoliberal approaches to development, as much as, if not more than, representing tools for democratic transformation (Mayo and Craig, 1995). International agencies such as the World Bank were opening up new spaces for the voluntary and community sectors, bringing NGOs into the policy development process through the World Bank Inspection Panel, for example (Clark et al, 2003). But these initiatives have been described as representing part of wider strategies to promote 'cost-effective' solutions to the problems of increasing poverty, polarisation and social exclusion, worldwide, within the neoliberal development paradigm (Fiorini, 2000). To what extent could citizens actually make any difference then? This is a question with considerable implications for the development professional. Although this chapter focuses on British professionals' experiences, the final section returns to some of the parallels between their dilemmas and those experienced by those working in international development contexts.

Modernisation: unpacking the underlying assumptions

Modernisation, in the British context, has been closely associated with New Labour, with its emphasis on the need for change, if Britain is to keep pace in the global context. What, then, has this all been about? Government itself has pointed to the importance of modernisation as a response to changes in the global economy. As Britain is increasingly integrated into the global economy, it is argued, so competitiveness becomes increasingly important as a factor affecting domestic policy choices (Prime Minister's Strategy Unit, 2007). If Britain is to retain its competitiveness, in this context, then public services have to be modernised, to be increasingly competitive too. They need to be leaner and more cost-efficient as well as more responsive to an increasingly articulate and demanding public, users with rising expectations, many of whom expect public services to come up to the same standards as they expect from private sector companies. Social democratic models of the welfare state require modernisation in any case, it has been argued, to render them fit for purpose, breaking away from the view that 'one size fits all', replacing what has been described as the 'producer culture', with a new consumer culture, with tailor-made services 'geared to the needs of users not the convenience of producers' (DH, 2000, para 2.12).

Social policy theorists have explored this imperative to reform over the past decade (Newman, 2001; Miller, 2004; Taylor-Gooby et al, 2005). The end result, it has been argued, in summary, has been to shift the very basis of the welfare state in Britain, away from a predominantly social democratic model which aimed to mitigate and indeed to challenge the worst excesses of capitalism to a more pragmatic 'Third Way', seeking to ensure that the welfare state operates in a way that 'complements, rather than conflicts with economic imperatives' (Page, 2007, p 19), contributing to the economic goal of competitiveness in a more open national economy.

Now aspects of this drive for reform can actually be traced through the policies of previous governments. The emphasis on rolling back the state was central to the aims of what Fitzpatrick has described as 'modern conservatism', the broad spectrum of thought underpinning the Thatcher/Major governments (Fitzpatrick, 2005). In summary, these approaches have rested on assumptions about the superiority of laissez-faire capitalism. According to neoliberals, markets are considered to be more efficient in terms of the allocation of resources and the maximisation of individual freedom and choice. Markets make the world go round effectively, whether locally or globally – or both – although neoconservatives and the Christian Right have also pointed to the need 'to restrain the destructive tendencies of liberal modernity with an important role for government still, in terms of 'upholding morals, behaviour, faith, belief and knowledge' (Fitzpatrick, 2005, p 7). While there have been and continue to be tensions between the more neoliberal and the more neoconservative wings of modern conservatism, there are, then, common threads.

Social democratic versions of the welfare state came under attack from modern conservatives on a number of grounds. These included allegations of the wasteful use of resources, which could be more effectively deployed via the private sector, exacerbated by the self-interest of professionals and bureaucrats within the public services, and the promotion of a dependency culture, undermining individuals' responsibility for themselves and their families. As one of the welfare state's most strident critics, Charles Murray argued that public welfare had resulted in perverse effects, such as undermining family values by rewarding single parenthood and reducing work incentives by offering financial incentives to stay on benefits (Murray, 1984).

Although Murray came to focus on the moral dimensions of single motherhood as a key factor to be addressed, his analysis began from the assumption that individuals were rational actors, economic men and women, calculating the costs and benefits of different financial incentives and acting accordingly. This assumption takes the argument to the core of neoliberalism. Underlying neoliberalism is the view that individuals are motivated by rational calculations of their own self-interest and that of their families, preserving their genes for the future, in a Social Darwinian struggle for the survival of the fittest, *The Selfish Gene*, as Dawkins expressed it (1976). In extreme form, as argued by the economist Hayek (1982), for example, far from selfishness representing a challenge to society, it is people's pursuit of their self-interests that will be of ultimate benefit to everyone, with greater dynamism in the economy and greater freedom, ultimately, and choice for all.

There is not the space to develop the counter-arguments here. In summary, it has been argued that this represents an extremely impoverished view of human beings. Far from being purely self-interested, human beings are also social animals, with emotions and sometimes irrational responses, too. Even in the world of work, a range of motivations beyond the desire for financial reward drives people. For example, people view retirement in differing ways, over and above the key financial implications (Vickerstaff, 2006). Summarising the findings of previous research McNair concluded that 'work is good for people, and that generally people like work, but want more control over what they do and how they do it' (McNair, 2006, p 486). The benefits of work could include companionship, for example, and a sense of being able to make a contribution to society. His study of the older labour market found that 91% of those employed agreed with the statement that, 'I enjoy working with my colleagues' as did 92% of those who had retired, while only 17% of those employed and 15% of those retired agreed with the statement that 'I do not feel my work makes a contribution to society' (McNair, 2006, p 491).

The point to emphasise here is simply this. Despite being so contentious, the neoliberal view of human motivation has been and continues to exert a powerful influence on public policy. Human beings, according to this view, are both rational and self-interested, needing to be managed, accordingly, with a combination of sticks and carrots. Modernisation agendas typically start from such premises.

Consistency and inconsistency in New Labour's modernisation of public services

So what is new about 'New Labour'? Without going into the already extensive literature on the nature of the New Labour project, for the purposes of this book, several features need to be emphasised. The outcomes of Labour's public service reforms have been summarised as business being more firmly embedded than ever in social policy, as the welfare state has been adapted to 'both the articulated and perceived interests of business' (Farnsworth and Holden, 2006, p 492), combined with some powerful centralising and controlling features from central government. But this is far from providing the full story. Successive Labour governments have also given priority to tackling poverty and social exclusion (Alcock, 2006), with an emphasis on community engagement as well as a continuing emphasis on individual choice, just as they have emphasised the importance of partnership working and collaboration, albeit within the overall context of increasing competition within and between the private, statutory, voluntary and community sectors (Balloch and Taylor, 2001; Taylor, 2003).

The role of the community has been central here, both as the object and subject of public policies. The Social Exclusion Unit, set up in 1998, played a key role in developing and promoting area-based initiatives to develop joined-up solutions to the joined-up problems facing Britain's poorest communities (Alcock, 2006). For example, a range of initiatives with a particular focus on young people was developed to tackle issues defined as priorities, issues such as those associated with rough sleepers, truancy and school exclusions, teenage pregnancy and young runaways, together with an emphasis on holistic approaches to the more deprived neighbourhoods. To target regeneration towards these areas, the New Deal for Communities programme was established, with a focus on community participation and engagement, putting local people in the driving seat, as this was expressed in the public policy documents of the time.

What this might mean in practice remained to be explored, as residents in the most deprived neighbourhoods struggled to represent the varying priorities of different interests in their areas, while fulfilling targets already determined by central government. Government policies were simultaneously problematising and pathologising the subjects of welfare while enlisting them in the development and implementation of these new public policy agendas. Tracking the development of policies to tackle street homelessness, for example, Fitzpatrick and Jones argue that Labour's agendas have attempted to combine agendas for social justice with agendas for social cohesion and social control, with the latter set of policy objectives taking priority over the former – an outcome more likely, in their view, 'to undermine than promote the well-being of street homeless people' (Fitzpatrick and Jones, 2005, p 389).

Meanwhile, communities were to be directly involved in service delivery, with the third (that is, not-for-profit, voluntary and community) sector encouraged to engage alongside the statutory and private sectors, developing collaborative partnerships while competing for contracts. In an increasingly market-driven scenario for public service provision, collaborative partnerships and third sector involvement in service delivery could lend legitimacy, it could be argued, to the increasing marketisation of service delivery, overall. The point to emphasise here is simply this: communities in deprived areas and young people more generally were to be the focus for public policy interventions as well as active participants and partners (if not necessarily equal partners, of course). And the professionals working with them were charged with delivering these agendas, agents of competing messages from government while finding themselves subjected to modernising agendas for public service reform, as the allegedly self-interested producers of welfare in need of the disciplines of the market as well as the central state. This was indeed a mix of policy approaches and styles overall, as well as within and between the different services involved (Larsen et al, 2006).

Modernisation and public service professionals

How, then, have these modernisation agendas impacted on the public service professionals who have been tasked with the responsibility for implementing them? As this chapter has already suggested, modernisation agendas have been rooted in assumptions about human motivation, emphasising the importance of individual self-interest. While neoliberals point to the beneficial ways in which the actions of rational, self-interested individuals promote the effective workings of market economies, modernising governments identify more negative aspects, too. Left to themselves, it has been supposed, professionals pursue their self-interest, like any other interest group, promoting their producer interests to the detriment of public service consumers. Far from acting as knights in shining armour, in the public interest, professionals are just as, if not more, likely to act as knaves, continually pressing for increasing resources for public services, funded and delivered to meet their own occupational needs rather than the needs of their clients. Pursuing the chess analogy, as Chapter Five has already explained, Julian Le Grand has pointed to the alternative aims of the modernisation agenda, with the consumer as sovereign queen rather than passive pawn (Le Grand, 2003). From such perspectives then, professionals, along with public service bureaucrats, have been viewed with suspicion, if not downright distrust.

So modernisation agendas aim to increase the regulation of public service professionals. This is intended to maximise governmental control of resources, holding public spending in check while obtaining maximum value for money, reducing the scope for professional discretion, while continuing to expect professionals to adopt increasingly entrepreneurial ways of working, to meet the varying range of user wants and needs. The new public management (NPM) that was developed in the Thatcher/Major years set out to achieve these differing policy objectives. Public services were to compete through the introduction of quasi-markets and internal markets in the National Health Service (NHS), along with other forms of marketisation, including the promotion of public–private partnerships, arm's-length delivery agencies and the increasing use of contracting to the private, voluntary and community sectors.

Meanwhile, private sector models of management were to be introduced within the public sector itself, as part of modernising drives to increase efficiency (particularly cost-efficiency). NPM was, in addition, aimed at promoting innovation and enterprise, thereby improving the quality of services and their responsiveness to the ever more varied and demanding requirements of consumers. The characteristics of this NPM strategy to import private sector management approaches have included both tighter definitions of measures and standards of performance, with greater emphasis on performance management to achieve clearly specified targets and an increasing emphasis on entrepreneurialism, breaking up monolithic units into smaller cost centres, with enhanced responsibilities for financial management. Increasing centralisation has been accompanied by elements of decentralisation, something of a paradox perhaps with accompanying dilemmas for the professionals involved (Bottery, 1998; Exworthy and Halford, 1999; Clarke et al, 2000).

"Decentralisation – what decentralisation?", as one professional put this, reflecting on the dilemmas of attempting to develop programmes to address local priorities while ensuring that centrally determined targets were met. Another reflected:

'The shift away from locally determined need to centrally determined need, the shift from local authorities which I work for, having more responsibility and power to determine where they spend resources, that's shifted over the last decade to a place where much of the resources I have responsibility for now, are targeted from central government or they're geared to central government objectives. So that's been a major shift.' (Quoted in Mayo et al, 2007a)

It has been argued that since the election of Labour governments from 1997, NPM has been taken further. There has been increasing emphasis on the audit culture, regulating professionals more tightly through pressures to achieve ever more precisely defined targets. Resources have been increasingly tied to specific short-term initiatives, as in the case of so many programmes to promote area regeneration. Increasingly, unqualified or semi-qualified staff, perhaps cheaper and less independent than their professional counterparts, have provided front-line services, leaving the latter to the more specifically managerial tasks of resource management, risk management and quality control (Causer and Exworthy, 1999; Saks and Allsop, 2007).

Supporters have argued that Labour's strategies for modernisation have the potential for moving beyond commodification to democratisation. Critics, in contrast, have pointed to their unevenness and internal contradictions, with their increasing emphasis on consumerism potentially leading to regimes of surveillance (Newman and Vidler, 2006), for service consumers as well as for service providers. Reflecting on the impact of an over-emphasis on the use of market forces, such as the promotion of competitiveness via performance-related pay, Richard Layard has pointed to the potentially negative effects on professional motivation. By upping financial incentives, he suggests, we may actually 'diminish a person's internal incentives to give of his [sic] best and to live up to the name of his profession' (Layard, 2005, p 159). He goes on to argue that '[T]he professional ethic is a precious motivation that should be cherished' (2005, p 159). And, as Clarke, Smith and Vidler have argued, 'Managing the volatile intersection of needs, choices, resources and competing priorities will remain a site of intense emotional labour' (Clarke et al, 2006, p 332). They go on to suggest that far from making the consumer sovereign, Labour's choice agenda is about populist anti-elitism. It is, in addition, they suggest, about persuading middle-class service users not to go completely private as well as being a proxy for competition and marketisation more generally, leaving front-line professionals to cope as best they can with the competing pressures that result.

Marketisation and community governance

As this chapter has already suggested, user/consumer and community engagement has been a key feature of the modernisation agenda. The emphasis is on service provision to meet the increasingly diverse requirements of rational self-interested consumers, along with an emphasis on putting the community in the driving seat when it comes to Labour strategies for area-based regeneration – all within the context of increasing pressures to meet targets tightly defined by central government. Unsurprisingly, the results have been challenging, both for the communities and the often-competing interests within and between communities and neighbourhoods. The results have been challenging for those working with them on the front line, community and youth workers, along with a range of professionals with a 'community engagement' brief, economic development officers, planners, housing officers and health promotion workers, to name some of the most obvious.

There is an extensive literature on the challenges and dilemmas associated with small area-based attempts to tackle structural problems such as poverty and social deprivation, just as there is an extensive literature on the challenges associated with community engagement (Loney, 1983; Popple, 1995; Taylor, 2003). 'The uneasy relationship between community development work and the local state is a recurrent theme', as Banks and Orten have demonstrated in their study of the impact of modernisation on community development workers tasked with promoting this while facilitating community participation and active citizenship (Banks and Orten, 2005, p 97). As Chapter Three has already demonstrated, professionals concerned with the promotion of community engagement have typically found themselves working both *In and Against the State* (London Edinburgh Weekend Return Group, 1980), striving to persuade service providers to listen, while struggling to enable the different voices within neighbourhoods to be heard, women as well as men, minority communities including newcomers as well as established residents, younger people as well as older residents. Communities are rarely homogeneous. Too often, efforts to engage service users fail to reach beyond the so-called 'usual suspects', 'godfathers and godmothers', 'community stars' who may or may not represent wider interests in their neighbourhoods. And conversely, too often, decision makers decide who is and who is not representative on the basis of the extent to which particular individuals pose challenges for them – the troublesome citizens (Anastacio et al, 2000; Taylor, 2003).

Meanwhile, community representatives have been faced with an often bewildering array of structures of governance, each with their targets and their particular jargons: local strategic partnerships, CENs, New Deal for Communities boards, community safety partnerships and a range of service user forums for health and social services, to name but a few. A recent study sponsored by the Joseph Rowntree Foundation identified the processes by which individuals can become entrapped, identified as active citizens in their communities and so invited to participate in a spiralling whirl of different meetings, unless they burn out first. Tellingly the report was titled *Community Participation: Who Benefits?* (Skidmore et al, 2006). While there has been increasing recognition of the need for capacity building to enable citizens to engage with these structures of governance effectively, this, 'as with other dimensions of anti-poverty action, is a long-term challenge' (Alcock, 2006, p 245). So is the contradiction between long-term investments and short-term strategies (and funding regimes).

In summary, then, professionals working in these contexts are being expected to balance these competing pressures, in addition to the pressures already outlined above, the pressures associated with competing wants and needs in an increasingly marketised policy framework. They are being expected to facilitate the implementation of an uneasy mix of policy goals, tackling social exclusion while curtailing public expenditure, all within the context of the third way's aim to transform the relationship between the state, the market and civil society (Banks and Orten, 2005). And front-line professionals are being expected to motivate citizens to participate in increasingly complex structures of governance, combating their understandable cynicism, in neighbourhoods that have experienced one regeneration initiative after another, and programmes to promote decentralisation are counterbalanced, in practice, from the centre.

For some front-line professionals, modernisation agendas come to be seen as challenging the very basis of their professional role, prioritising the achievement of short-term objectives over and above the longer-term processes of building relationships for sustainable community development. Increasingly, as one professional with many years experience of working within the voluntary sector commented, "my job was about coordinating, managing organisations" (quoted in Mayo et al, 2007a) in a climate of increasing competition for small pots of money and increasing competition for legitimacy, within and between voluntary and community sector organisations. The result was 'quite stark' in this professional's view, "who got money and who had [influence] and where the power was held", with a 'new brutalism' emerging, in the process. As another front-line professional reflected, "The contract culture breeds competition ... there is a danger that the voluntary sector could lose its unique selling points in the process" (quoted in Mayo et al, 2007a, p 676).

Contradictions of modernisation: working with young people

Working with young people has provided particular examples of these challenges and professional dilemmas. The impact of nearly a decade of rapid change, it has been argued, has been 'to cause anxiety and stress for those working with young people', leading them 'to question their sense of identity' (Oliver, 2006, p 6). 'If New Labour were a teenager', Davies has argued even more forcibly, 'its behaviour as a youth policy-maker would surely by now have attracted some of that "intensive support" so strongly advocated by *Youth Matters*' (Davies, 2005, p 21). Davies goes on to suggest that the government had been exhibiting signs of obsessive-compulsive behaviour, even paranoia, in its preoccupation with young people's potential for anti-social behaviour, with youth as the dangerous 'Other' (Davies, 2005, p 21). Alternatively, Davies suggested, bipolar disorder might be a more appropriate diagnosis, given the contrasts between policies for the containment of 'feral youth' on the one hand, and policies for the support of deserving youth, young consumers in need of individually tailored services and enjoyable places in which to spend their leisure time on the other. Reflecting on the most recent proposals, as set out in *Youth Matters*, Davies went on to question whether youth workers would end up asking 'Where is the youth work?' in all this, if present at all (Davies, 2005, p 25).

In summary, then, youth policies have exhibited key traits of modernisation policies more generally, top-down policies from central government including strong emphases on social control accompanied by centrally controlled targets for outputs. This was all within the context of an emphasis on increasing participation and choice for young people as individual consumers, while the problems of social exclusion among young people were set out by the Social Exclusion Unit's report *Bridging the Gap: New Opportunities for 16-18 year olds Not in Education, Employment or Training* (1999). This framework of policies set out to promote social inclusion through preparation to meet the needs of employers tackling poor school attendance, poor school performance and the consequent failure to acquire relevant qualifications and skills. As this report argued, 'The best defence against social exclusion is having a job, and the best way to get a job is to have a good education, with the right training and experience' (Social Exclusion Unit, 1999, p 6).

New Labour, it has been suggested, 'has always been ambivalent in its policies towards young people', with 'four different, sometimes overlapping approaches to youth work' (Moon, 2005, p 30). Moon went on to list these as the 1998 Criminal Disorder Act introducing ASBOs, the introduction of the Connexions Service (in 2000) to provide coordinated advice and support, targeting young people not in employment, education or training (NEETs), the Transforming Youth Work Agenda (in 2001) and the 2004 Children Act bringing services for children together. These four were then followed by the fifth, the Green Paper *Youth Matters* (DES, 2005) and the government's response to the consultation *Youth Matters: Next Steps* (DES, 2006).

Youth Matters has been criticised for conceptualising young people as individual consumers in the marketplace for services. In the view of Jeffs and Smith, for example, this was 'part of an effort to reorient state-sponsored (and if possible non-state sponsored) work with young people' (Jeffs and Smith, 2006, p 25). Ideologically driven, the core aim, in their view, was 'to change the ethos of provision; to fundamentally alter the ways in which young people relate to the state and the market; to realign provision by changing from a membership to a consumerist model of youth work; to "marketwise" delivery so that youth work, like schools, reinforces and confirms for young people a particular understanding of the world and their place in it. Such an understanding', they concluded, 'rejects earlier traditions inherited from a liberal education and welfarist ethos and supplants them with a view that holds the market as sacred and immutable' (Jeffs and Smith, 2006, p 25).

More specifically, the proposal that young people should have Opportunity Cards has come in for particular criticism. The proposed cards were presented as facilitating freedom of choice, young people being enabled to use the cards to purchase leisure services from a range of providers – locating young people in the role of consumer, it has been argued, and greatly enhancing the potential for charging. Critics such as Jeffs and Smith have objected to this process of marketisation, going on to raise further concerns about the potential invasion of privacy and individual freedom, with increased scope for the surveillance and monitoring of young people. In the context of debates on the use of ASBOs, very particularly, although not of course exclusively, targeted at young people, this potential extension of surveillance has given rise to anxieties that the government has been effectively labelling far too many young people as criminals, or at least as potential criminals, all in the name of increasing freedom and individual choice. The use of ASBOs for teenagers has come in for particular criticism including by Martin Narey, former head of the prison and probation service who resigned in 2005.

Parallels have been drawn between agendas for criminal justice (including specific proposals for dealing with young offenders in Scotland) and another particularly contentious aspect of youth work policies, the issue of the curriculum (Barr, 2005). This has been the subject of considerable debate, welcomed, or at least accepted as inevitable, by some, but extensively criticised by others. Attempts to introduce a curriculum for youth work were mooted in the Thatcher years in the wake of the introduction of the National Curriculum in schools. Jeffs noted that, 'Some, certainly not all, youth work managers and workers predicted that a centralising, right-wing government, determined to curb the autonomy of professionals', would sooner or later impose a national curriculum on youth work (Jeffs, 2004, p 56). It was not the Conservatives, however, but 'a centralising Labour government determined to curb the autonomy of professionals and turn back the progressive tide of the 1960s' (Jeffs, 2004, p 56).

More recent curriculum proposals have been the subject of criticism for fundamentally shifting the balance of youth work away from informal education, with the emphasis on bottom-up processes and relationship building, towards a top-down emphasis on the imposition of centrally controlled targets for outputs, the very opposite of youth work's ethos on voluntary participation and empowerment. There are parallels, here, it has been argued, with policy changes in the criminal justice system, which has been criticised for becoming more 'top-down', more centralised and more target-orientated – and more punitive (Barr, 2005). In both cases too, Barr suggests, national standards 'place unnecessarily rigid boundaries on professional discretion' and 'encourage a tick-box mentality amongst workers', rather than building dialogue between the worker and the young person (Barr, 2005, p 24).

How, then, has modernisation been impacting on professionals working with young people? Young people's rights have emerged on policy agendas in Britain, and more widely internationally, particularly since the 1989 United Nations Convention on the Rights of the Child. Children and young people have the right to care, just as they have the right to health and education along with the right to protection from exploitation and abuse. The four core principles of the Convention are non-discrimination; devotion to the best interests of the child; the right to life, survival and development; and respect for the views of the child. Children and young people have the right to have their voices heard, a right that youth workers have emphasised in their work to promote young people's participation and empowerment. This sits somewhat uneasily alongside aspects of current policies towards young people in Britain.

Youth workers have been working within this policy framework, doing a job that has been described as 'challenging and stressful' in any case, 'a marginal group of professionals, unsure of their own status and position, in a poorly paid and insufficiently funded service' (Moon, 2005, p 29), although strongly motivated, in many cases in Moon's research, by a 'burning desire' to make a difference. The impact of government over the past 10 years has been identified as causing 'anxiety and confusion for many working in the field and to lead them to question their sense of professional identity' (Oliver, 2006, p 5). Where, as Davies (2005) has asked, is the youth work in all this?

Youth workers who were interviewed in our study expressed mixed views on these issues. Aspects of modernisation, such as increased accountability, were not necessarily rejected; some aspects were even welcomed, particularly if they were perceived as leading to improved service delivery. As one experienced youth worker reflected, although there was always a degree of accountability, "we're more answerable now ... so yeah, and it's stats driven which is a good thing ..." (quoted in Mayo et al, 2007a, p 673). Recognition of the need to meet targets as part of formal accountability procedures emerged as a potentially positive feature from a number of interviews. The problem was that some of the least readily quantifiable aspects of the job were also among the most valuable – and the most at risk of being under-valued, as a result of being less readily measurable.

Concluding her discussion of the extent to which youth and community workers continue to exercise autonomy and discretion within the context of modernisation and NPM, Fitzsimons quotes a worker himself quoting Walt Whitman: 'Contradictions? I contain multitudes of them', ending with a saying from Berthold Brecht, 'In the contradiction lies the hope' (Fitzsimons, 2007, p 56). More detailed discussion of how front-line professionals cope with the contradictions of modernisation is the subject of the subsequent chapter.

NINE

Doing the work: negotiating the modernisation agenda

The modernisation of community

As previous chapters have already argued, modernisation agendas define spatial and other communities both as part of the problems of exclusion and community cohesion in contemporary Britain and as part of their solution. Communities are defined as constituting social problems, when neighbourhoods become characterised as sites for 'out of control' young people, for cycles of deprivation and for conflictual community relations. And conversely, neighbourhoods are being defined as vehicles for public sector reform, invited to step into the democratic deficit that has been associated with the emasculation of local government and the destruction of the social fabric that so often accompanies rapid economic change. Thus, it has been suggested, communities become the harbingers of devolved community governance and the new 'localism', espoused by political parties across the political spectrum. As Chapter Two has already suggested, these differing definitions, approaches and agendas have impacted in powerful ways, posing ethical issues and dilemmas for front-line professionals working to promote participation in governance, active citizenship and empowerment among service users and among young people, particularly those living within disadvantaged neighbourhoods, identified as being in need of some form of professional intervention.

There are powerful parallels with decentralisation strategies pursued in development contexts in the South. As Greig, Hulme and Turner have demonstrated, 'One of the most popular initiatives for reducing democratic deficits has been decentralization involving the delegation of decision-making authority from central government to political bodies in provinces, municipalities, communes and other subnational territories' (Greig et al, 2007, p 229). Dubbed the latest fashion in development administration from the 1980s, this approach gained momentum from the 1990s, in the wake of the collapse of the former Soviet Union and the end of a number of military dictatorships in the global South. Decentralisation strategies were typically accompanied by the promotion of community participation, with enhanced roles for NGOs, including international NGOs (INGOs), as well as more local community-based organisations (CBOs). Here too, then, the democratic deficit was to be addressed. And state intervention was to be rolled back, with NGOs/INGOs providing legitimacy, representing the acceptable face of increasing marketisation (Hulme and Edwards, 1997; Mayo, 2005). Community participation has been described as a new orthodoxy, the 'new tyranny' even in the context of the neoliberal development paradigm (Cooke and Kothari, 2001; Hickey and Mohan, 2004).

There are also powerful parallels in terms of the implications for INGOs, NGOs, CBOs and those who work within them. There are inherent tensions in their roles (both nationally and internationally in relation to international structures of governance such as the World Bank and the International Monetary Fund) – 'Too close for comfort?', it has been suggested, raising questions about the extent to which they can maintain their independence, as INGOs collaborate ever more closely with the institutions of global capital (Hulme and Edwards, 1997). And there are similar tensions in relation to issues of democratic accountability (the 'lap-top' NGO, or the 'non-governmental individual', as some of the less representative organisations have been dubbed), tensions that have been exacerbated in the context of neoliberal development agendas, globally. Operating within this context as they do, INGOs and local NGOs are themselves the objects of modernisation as well as its potential subjects. As a consequence, the profession is subject to similar contradictory pressures, pressures that include the increasing use of NPM approaches, as organisations strive to demonstrate their cost-effectiveness in achieving outputs as they compete for funding from international donors.

Having outlined these shared challenges, this chapter moves on to examine the ways in which front-line professional workers are able to keep doing effective development work *despite* the contradictions of public policies. How do different front-line professionals themselves define the issues, tensions and potential dilemmas inherent in their development roles? How do they respond to attempts to managerialise the job? Which aspects of NPM are actually being welcomed? As Chapter Two has already indicated, greater accountability, for example, is being actively welcomed, in some contexts. We also explore which aspects of NPM are being identified as particularly challenging to professional identities and ethics, resisted in some cases, whether actively or more passively, via strategies of 'strategic compliance'. What coping strategies are these professionals developing and what sources of support do they draw on in response to these challenges? Are new forms of professionalism emerging in response to NPM, or are they becoming increasingly at risk of de-professionalisation? This chapter concludes by reflecting on issues of professionalisation, asking whether the profession is reaching a 'tipping point' beyond which development work becomes no more than a form of project management in an environment where workers and agencies are increasingly fragmented and divided.

Ethical challenges of modernisation

Like professional social workers and youth workers (Banks, 1995, 1999), community workers and other front-line professionals may expect to face more ethical issues and dilemmas as professional values come under pressure from:

* increasing marketisation and NPM;
* increased fragmentation and competition between communities and community groups in local areas;
* increasing pressures for consumer rights and user-/community-determined priorities on the one hand and the requirements for rationing scarce resources on the other;
* increasing decentralisation of responsibilities without necessarily being accompanied by commensurate powers and resources;
* increasing pressures for centralised controls of targets and outputs; and
* increasing pressures to work across professional boundaries, involving varying codes and practices.

Faced with all these challenges, Freidson (2001) has argued, professionals need to start with a knowledge and critical understanding of ethical issues, and then to have the time and safe space for reflection/self-reflection along with professional supervision and both managerial and non-managerial support. These are in addition to the resources that they themselves bring to the job due to their own personal history, upbringing, cultural mores, motivation and professional commitment. Together, these should help them to cope most effectively and with the least anxiety and guilt (Bailey and Schwartzberg, 1995). It has been suggested that without these coping mechanisms professionals are at increasing risk of burnout.

Previous chapters have already demonstrated that irrespective of modernisation, community development work involves inherent tensions (Craig et al, 1982; Loney, 1983; Popple, 1995). Community workers have been described as insiders as well as outsiders: 'In and Against the State' in previous terminology (London Edinburgh Weekend Return Group, 1980), negotiating and facilitating bridges within and between communities and the agencies responsible for addressing their needs. There are inherent tensions here as well as potential strengths – and spaces for creative practice. Having strong roots in the community has been identified as a source of legitimacy when negotiating with formal organisations – a source of strength when negotiating for service improvements, for example (Mayo et al, 2007a). But in the current context of the new localism, with responsibilities being increasingly passed down the line to communities – without necessarily including the requisite resources – development workers are facing new challenges as they engage with managing forms of 'indirect rule' (systems of apparent devolution, but hedged effectively with requirements and constraints from above). Hiving off policy implementation effectively depoliticises issues that should arguably be resolved democratically and transparently, leaving workers to cope with the resulting anxieties as best they can, as they attempt to deal with intractable policy conflicts which get passed down the line from government (Hoggett, 2005a).

Meanwhile, the changing boundaries between sectors in an increasingly marketised economy of welfare would seem to be exacerbating the pressures on front-line professionals. Some of the most painful dilemmas recounted related to the tensions arising *within* the voluntary/community sector. For example, the previous chapter included participants' references to the 'brutalism' that can occur when voluntary/community sector agencies compete for resources, fighting for their own organisational survival in the context of increasingly short-term contracts and casualised labour. Others highlighted the dilemmas inherent in being a public service sector worker feeling blamed for the shortcomings of the public sector in its entirety by their counterparts in the voluntary sector, who present themselves as the only true representatives of the community while pursuing competing agendas for their own organisational survival. While the role of insider/outsider may have its potential advantages, this would seem less evident with the role of scapegoat/public enemy number one – without the right of reply.

The role involves inherent tensions, issues and dilemmas too, when it comes to defining professional boundaries. Many of these dilemmas have been seen to be increasing in the current policy context (Mayo et al, 2007a). Such dilemmas could be compounded if issues of 'race' and/or social class were also involved (for example, young black residents/employees being managed by white middle-class professionals answerable to adults in the community as well as to funding bodies). Dilemmas associated with the boundaries of 'race' and class emerged very powerfully from our research. For example, black workers spoke of the difficulties when white managers failed to address the issues that they raised, including disciplinary issues involving other black workers. Managers (and local politicians) could be so nervous about possible allegations of racism, it was suggested, that they could be reluctant to pursue personnel issues involving black staff, even if black team leaders were raising these issues. Conversely too, there were instances of black workers expressing frustration, feeling undervalued and undermined by white managers.

Working in partnerships across sectors and across organisational and professional boundaries adds further complexity to these potential challenges and dilemmas. There is a growing literature on the problems associated with partnership working including the tensions associated with relationships and inequalities of power (Balloch and Taylor, 2001; Glendinning et al, 2002; Taylor, 2003). Front-line professionals may feel particularly vulnerable in this context, potentially caught between the competing pressures of official agencies and the differing interests that are being articulated – or not being articulated – within communities.

From the perspectives of participants in our study, partnership working also emerged as particularly problematic, in that the professionals involved could find themselves effectively having to cope 'on their own'. For example, one participant gave a (highly confidential) account of her dilemmas when another agency consistently failed to deliver to the partnership, as promised. The participant came to understand the complex reasons for this block, but felt unable to address these. Taking the issue up formally via her line manager could simply jeopardise the fragile relations between the agencies in question. So the worker felt that she had no option but to cope as best she could, on her own (Mayo et al, 2007c, p 144).

Moving towards de-professionalisation – or working towards a new professionalism?

In the face of current challenges, there are differing possibilities for public service professions such as community and youth work, according to Banks (2004, p 123), including working towards 'a new professionalism', with more stress on social justice agendas, anti-discriminatory practice, client/user participation and working across professional boundaries to raise service provision in the most deprived areas up to national norms. Alternatively, however, Banks points to the risks of de-professionalisation, with a narrowing of the scope for professional judgement and an undermining of trust and public service morale, as workers become subject to performance management regimes focused on demonstrating short-term outputs rather than the achievement of long-term and sustainable outcomes.

Such concerns about the impact of NPM mirror those about developments in other human service areas such as social care and nursing (Causer and Exworthy, 1999). While professional practice itself becomes increasingly focused on technical and managerial issues, unqualified or less qualified staff may be engaged in the direct face-to-face work. This may become further complicated in community engagement work, if less qualified staff are also local people, as is often the case. While the employment of local people does, of course, demonstrate possibilities for widening opportunities for local communities, this also raises challenges if local 'para professionals' remain less trained and less valued in their roles. Similarly, pressures for greater accountability can have contradictory effects, providing quality assurance, but in ways which may confuse 'giving an account' – completing statistical returns on time – with fuller approaches to democratic accountability (Hopwood and Miller, 1994).

Modernisation as progressive change: towards a 'new professionalism'?

For a significant minority of the respondents in our research, the current policy context was indeed perceived positively as offering professionals new opportunities to work more effectively in more decentralised and integrated ways. Neighbourhood Renewal, for example, was perceived as providing enhanced possibilities to work in innovative ways to improve service delivery, tackling key problems of education, employment, housing and community safety in deprived neighbourhoods. While the Neighbourhood Renewal programme does have set parameters that were potentially problematic, for some of our respondents it also provided spaces in which professionals could use their initiative. Such increased scope for flexibility and creativity was clearly valued by a number of our respondents. There is some evidence from our research that such positive opinions may be more characteristic of professionals who have previously been employed in relatively traditional, formal bureaucracies in the statutory sector, such as local authority housing or planning departments. As one professional with such previous experiences in local government, currently working on Neighbourhood Renewal, commented:

> '… the idea [of Neighbourhood Renewal] is to improve the experience of the lives of people who live in the poorest areas of the borough, in relation to education, employment, housing, crime, all those things…. The way to do that is to try and work in a different way. So it's about trying new things that have never been tried before … then (once good practice has been identified) to think about how that … can be mainstreamed in the way that service is delivered in the council. So that's basically the work that I'm aiming to do. It's very loose. Those are the parameters, but there are no specific guidelines within it. So it's very loose in terms of what you do, how you do it and everything. The only limitation is the fact that there is a budget that's been set. So that will restrict what you can do and how you can do it. But the idea of the budget for Neighbourhood Renewal is to draw on existing resources and this idea of mainstreaming. So that could be anything.'

This person went on to comment on the value of partnership working in development work as well as working across professional boundaries and with the local voluntary and community sectors as a mechanism for improving outcomes for local service users. Explaining the background to her views, she reflected on the sources of her own personal commitment to the policy goals of identifying new ways of improving services. As a black woman who had grown up in an area that was now being described as a deprived neighbourhood, she explained that:

> 'I want to make a difference to people's lives … because of my own personal experience of being born and growing up in this country and … the history going back to my parents as to why they were here anyway and the experiences that we had, you know.'

As a professional working in the statutory sector she added that:

> 'I've got first hand experience of what it's like to be working within those statutory frameworks … I wanted to make a difference for people [including] in the statutory things

> because I'm part of it ... I want to make a difference there ... change this bit of practice it's going to improve that person's life.'

Because of this background and personal commitment – a commitment that was deeply rooted in her own values and experiences – she reflected that she felt able to translate central policies into decentralised initiatives with real benefits for local people:

> 'In terms of my own personal thing, I think that's the driver for me – to always ... look at where these initiatives are coming from, essentially from government, what they are saying, and then through the work that I can do, locally, with the projects or with other things, or just from my own personal experience [I can] identify the real problem [as this relates to individuals' needs] – [translating the issue] into statutory agency language ... [relating] national targets and the local plans ... so that their [that is, statutory sector] action then will have a direct impact and improve that person's situation in the locality.'

More contentious aspects of modernisation: towards de-professionalisation?

To be effective, development requires a role with discretionary autonomy and one that takes the long view in forming decisions and making interventions. Currently, such work is undertaken within a framework of centrally defined targets, priorities and resources, alongside intensive forms of accountability. Our participants were not inherently hostile to either targets or accountability and sometimes saw these as potentially helpful in securing improved service provision and welcomed them in the context of an under-supported and under-managed role. However, narrow output-focused over-regulation suffocated the capacity for discretionary autonomy and reduced the role to that of 'apparatchik', denied the long view and ultimately drained the passion and emotional commitments so essential to it. Despite attempts to protect their discretionary autonomy, often by seeking as yet unregulated areas of activity, and to maintain a long view, our participants were fearful that current policy directions would lead to worsening service outcomes.

While there were positive comments on the opportunities for improving services in the context of the changing balance between centralisation and decentralisation, the much more widely held view was that the balance had shifted decisively towards the former. Indeed several of our respondents questioned the very notion of decentralisation. They argued the contrary, that NPM was reducing the scope for professional judgement and undermining professional identities, values and morale. An experienced and senior professional who was responsible for young people's programmes within a local authority put this very forcibly:

'The shift away from locally determined need to centrally determined need, the shift from local authorities which I work for, having had more responsibility and power to determine where they spend resources, that's shifted over the last decade to a place where much of the resources I have a responsibility for now, are targeted from central government or they're geared to central government objectives. So that's been a major shift.'

There were increasing difficulties, he suggested, in maintaining genuine accountability downwards as well as satisfying the requirements of formal accountability upwards. Central direction threatened the very purpose of development work:

'… determining what that end should be, I think. I mean that's why we want to get young people … to do – and adults – to determine what they think the end should be. Then they need to move towards that. But of course there are other much more pragmatic pressures around … I mean the major shift in local authority funding over the last decade, it may be longer now, two decades really, has been the shift from local determination to national determination of resources, you know … money being removed from the local and kind of put back in, recycled in such a way through regeneration … the pot that delivers, call it what you will.'

Decentralisation might be taken to imply the decentralisation of power and control, although this was not at all how the realities were perceived by many of the professionals in our study. In parallel, NPM agendas emphasise the importance of consumer- rather than producer-led services, putting the service user/consumer first. The reality, as this was experienced by many of the professionals in our study, was that there was indeed greater emphasis on accountability, but this was primarily defined in terms of accountability upwards rather than downwards, to programme funders and to central government rather than to service users and communities.

While professionals expressed serious reservations about aspects of NPM, however, it should be emphasised that none rejected the importance of accountability per se. Indeed, as we have seen, a number of those we talked to explicitly recognised that there had been a need for more effective accountability in the past. In this, they were reflecting their commitment to Banks' 'new professionalism' with greater accountability downwards via enhanced client/user participation.

For example, an experienced youth worker, who had worked in both the voluntary and statutory sectors, commented that although the youth service was skilled at working with young people,

> '... we weren't disciplined and that was our downfall. We'd go out, do [the] work, no write up and move on. So ... we suffered as a result [because the value of the work was not recognised]. But now we're having to [keep proper records and meet formal accountability requirements] ... the work [was] always answerable ... but ... we're more answerable on paper now [we have to be], we write reports and stats and all of that.'

This was a positive development in his view. He went on to qualify this, however, explaining that some of the most valuable aspects of youth work were not readily quantifiable, a point we made earlier in Chapter Four:

> 'We can work with a person for five hours but they're in need of those five hours because if ... they become homeless you need to take them to [the] Housing [Department] ... [or] to homeless units. If they're under age, social services get involved. All those different bits ... so you can spend probably more than five hours at times caring about [that one individual]. And the stats ... you won't see that side. You'll just see five hours spent face-to-face with one person. But the difference you've made in that person's life is important to the community and quite cheap, yeah.'

This recognition of the need to meet targets as part of formal accountability procedures emerged from a number of the interviews and group discussions, together with the view that these statistics were not necessarily measuring the most important aspects of the development role. For the majority, what was key was to provide the data to satisfy formal accountability procedures without sacrificing the more qualitative aspects of the development role, thereby retaining a professional commitment to accountability downwards and working to meet the needs and priorities of individuals and communities. A professional community development officer, working with a CEN, made similar points:

> 'When it comes down to monitoring and evaluation, there's loads of pressure I think to hit the outputs and things like that. But I think within the Community Network, it is more about the qualitative outcomes ... if we look at performance management systems and things like that ... I think there's a lot of scope for us defining the terms and delivering those outcomes. If we look at the Community Network and its performance, we're sort of out-performing on what they expect from us. And I think that allows us to get on with some of the larger, more qualitative issues, if we're talking about social change.'

We find the term 'strategic compliance' helpful to describe the many ways in which professional workers in our study developed strategies for satisfying as quickly as possible what were often regarded as the irrational or even absurd reporting requirements attending some government funding streams. These strategies were often being developed by those with a community development/youth and community work background – professionals with a long tradition of working on the boundaries. However, those from different professional formations seemed to be adopting similar strategies. Like many other professionals they have become adept in the art of impression management – ticking the boxes, cutting and pasting extracts from one grant application or interim report into another and so on. While many shared such forms of strategic compliance there was also some recognition that such strategies were becoming more difficult to implement. As the experienced professional managing youth services commented:

> 'We've always been good at bending and shaping targets. I can take a target and bend it in such a way, I'm skilled at

> that, [bending it] in such a way I can continue the work
> that I want to do as well as the work that is required [for
> me] to do. So it's about negotiation and often it's about a
> compromise, [in] achieving a desired end.'

But he also commented that "It is harder [to do] now".

He went on to discuss the changing balance between outputs, outcomes and processes:

> 'I think the way you get there, the process, is just as
> important if not more important than the outcome. Now
> that is completely reversed from outside. Outcome first, how
> you get there really is not considered necessarily important.
> I still believe very strongly – the process is very important
> indeed. That is what people will carry with them, that is
> what the people we work with will hopefully in their own
> lives remember and learn from most is the process, not the
> outcome. They can decide their own outcome and make
> those decisions for themselves, but what we can do is support
> them through a process to get there in a way in which they
> will find respectful and valuable to them. They can learn for
> themselves. More and more the outcome/output-led work
> is becoming the norm, and process-led work is becoming
> less able to fund and support ... it's problematic.'

Once again this raises questions about potential contradictions inherent in current government policies in general and NPM more specifically. To what extent might managerial practices be undermining the very development strategies that government has been seeking to promote, including strategies to promote active citizenship, to build capacities and to strengthen social capital – as well as undermining the potential for the 'new professionalism'?

Taking the community out of the voluntary and community sectors

Many of our respondents spoke about what they perceived to be some of the destructive impacts of the modernisation agenda on the community sector itself. One respondent, who had spent many years working in a city's voluntary and community sectors and engaging with different regeneration programmes, noted:

'In those early years, when I came into the centre it was
... just after some major cuts in relation to the voluntary
sector, but the voluntary sector was fairly un-bureaucratised
still, and, and there was a lot of community campaigning
going on, and that was, I suppose, the sort of flavour of the
work that we were doing there ... I think that ... after
City Challenge when SRB [Single Regeneration Budget]
came online ... increasingly my job was about coordinating,
managing organisations.'

She contrasted this management role with the way that she felt that
she had been able to work in the past when:

'... I was able to do work in the field [in a way] that was
really exciting as well, for me, really exciting projects that I
felt were ... really transforming the people I was working
with, and also increasingly working at a kind of area
wide policy level, and interacting with the changes in the
regeneration policy as they were coming down.'

In contrast, community engagement work, in the current policy
framework offered less space for creativity or innovation, she argued,
being driven by top-heavy bureaucratic structures and managerial
requirements, shifting the role of 'development worker' towards the
role of an administrator. Far from promoting partnership working, this
professional, in common with a number of others, commented on the
negative effects of the 'contract culture' increasing competition for small
pots of money and greater competition for contracts and for legitimacy
more generally. As another experienced youth work manager put it:

'I can't stand it; I can't stand the beating each other up for
an extra couple of quid stuff that goes on.'

Several professionals referred to what they described as the 'new
brutalism' in this context – as the voluntary sector became increasingly
competitive. Similar points were made in the seminar bringing together
professionals from the two areas of study. Here it was argued that, "The
contract culture breeds competition" and "there is a danger that the
voluntary sector could lose its unique selling points in the process".
More specifically, there were a number of comments made about which
groups tended to gain and which lost out as a result of competitive
contexts. This was a source of tension and ethical dilemmas for the

professionals concerned. As the previously quoted professional with extensive experience in the voluntary sector commented:

> 'We were finding that, compared with how we'd been at the beginning ... there were fewer and fewer small black groups, ethnic minority groups involved in those discussions, involved in "the forum". There was a lot we had to look at in ourselves which never really got addressed as far as I was concerned. The organisation itself [be]came increasingly caught up in delivering these contracts and developing services, and less and less concerned with looking to see how it was actually meeting [the] needs of these local groups who were, really critical in terms of providing a route way for the most marginalised young people in the community.... Working with them, ethically for me was really important, and there seemed to be less, less willingness and less capacity in the organisation to do that. And I think in the [voluntary] sector – ... I had quite a good view of the sector being involved in the area-wide stuff that I was doing – it was quite stark, who got money and who had [influence], and where the power was held ... there were a number of quite powerful organisations who really kind of tended to control everything, and sort out the money, and I became increasingly jaded with that really.'

This particular professional subsequently left the organisation to work for a non-profit agency concerned with health promotion, on the grounds that this appeared to offer more space and freedom, in her view, to meet the requirements of the agency and its funding bodies without compromising her own values as a professional.

Modernisation, professionalisation, de-professionalisation and the public service ethos

Professionals expressed concerns about the managerialist encroachment on their values and professional ethos. And yet there were also expressions of concern about increasing professionalisation. This seeming paradox might be explained as representing two sides of the same coin – that of significant changes in the public service professions themselves. There were anxieties about whether the professional role was becoming increasingly bureaucratised, focusing on project management rather than the development role per se, drawing professionals away from those aspects that gave them the most personal satisfaction, the aspects that made their jobs 'so much more than a job'. In response to these perceived threats, there were a number of comments from experienced professionals who had developed strategies for holding on to the most personally satisfying aspects of their roles. As we saw in previous chapters, professionals working with young people, for example, explained that continuing to do some face-to-face work was essential, in this respect.

There were also concerns about the future of the professions in question, concerns about de-professionalisation in practice. These reflections included a number of comments to the effect that the next generation of professionals was "more career orientated". Although younger professionals still had commitment there was a danger, according to one experienced practitioner, that "we could certainly professionalise the service out of existence". He added that, "we could easily go down the line of excluding people for lack of formal qualifications, because the government was equating qualifications with ability", which, in his view, was not always necessarily the case. He went on to question what he saw as a form of "mock or pseudo professionalism", when workers were so concerned to deliver outputs that they failed to use their initiative and creativity, avoiding any possible risks, unable to learn from their own experiences, including their own mistakes. A number of professionals echoed similar fears. There were, in addition, fears that local volunteers and community activists were losing out on employment and promotion opportunities as a result of these processes of 'professionalisation'. There were inherent tensions and contradictions here – anxieties about de-professionalisation on the one hand, along with anxieties about the potential reduction in opportunities for employment for local people working as 'para' professionals in the front-line services on the other.

It was also suggested that (in the view of some managers) local activists who had become employed as community professionals, working in regeneration programmes, found greater difficulty in coping with shifts in managerial targets. This was in contrast with professional colleagues, recruited from outside the area, who were perceived as being less resistant to such shifts, as they were less directly affected by local pressures. Professionals recruited from outside might, in this respect, prove easier to manage, it was suggested, and the managerial tasks might be safer in their hands. Such a view would be consistent with Halford and Leonard's concerns that face-to-face care work – and by extension development work – was being devalued and left to less qualified (and lower paid) staff. This left the qualified career professionals to pursue more highly rewarded bureaucratic and managerial tasks (Halford and Leonard, 1999).

Fears were also expressed about working across professional boundaries. While there were positive benefits to cross-professional working, there were also risks attached. These included the risk that any particular professional ethos might be swallowed up in more bureaucratic ways of working, with less clearly defined professional cultures. Regeneration work is not perceived as a profession per se, in any case, so professionals have, perhaps, identified with their original professions (as youth and community workers, housing and planning officers, for instance). However, such identifications may have less relevance for newly recruited graduates, in the current context. Such potential challenges to the development and the maintenance of an appropriate professional ethos and commitment could be further compounded by the changing nature of the labour market, as jobs in the field of regeneration (as in so many others) tend to be 'flexible' and short term.

The next generation of professionals may be coming into this work with different expectations and criteria for evaluating their professional roles and values. This may depend on their differing formative experiences, their 'habitus' in Pierre Bourdieu's terms, the unique combination of the interactions between the individual social actor and his/her social environment. This raises further questions about the extent to which the next generation of professionals are likely to develop the social capital – the links and connections with other professionals as well as with the communities with whom they work – which has been identified as so important for their role (Mayo et al, 2007a). This particular study was too limited in size, with too few younger, less experienced participants, to provide clear evidence here. The younger, less experienced professionals who were interviewed, however, did express comparable levels of commitment, in terms of wanting to 'make a difference' although there was, perhaps, less clarity about how this might be translated into practice. This may perhaps reflect their differing biographies, values and professional identities formed in less certain times.

Maybe unsurprisingly, it was the more experienced professionals who were expressing concerns about the future prospects for professional identities and values. This theme emerged strongly from the individual interviews and was reinforced in the subsequent group discussions. As Banks has demonstrated, 'the form, content and function of codes of professional ethics changes over time and varies according to place and circumstances, as the historical/developmental view of the process of professionalisation would predict' (Banks, 2004, p 123). In other words, changes in professional identities and values are to be anticipated in any event, let alone in a period of such potentially significant restructuring. The key question then becomes the direction of change, whether towards a 'new professionalisation' or an increasing de-professionalisation, however this latter term is being conceptualised – as opening up new opportunities for paid work for local people and/or as reducing the scope for professional judgements based on a public service ethos and values.

In his study of the impact of flexible working on personal character, the personal consequences of work in the new capitalism, Richard Sennett raises disturbing questions (Sennett, 1998). The world of flexible working and short-term commitments, Sennett argues, is antithetical to the promotion of the values of trust, mutual responsibility and commitment. Sennett's book drew on studies of work in the private sector, however, while the participants in our study were working as professionals in the public, voluntary and community sectors. Their work was still clearly more than just a job. Despite the pressures of the contemporary context, their professional commitments were rooted in their personal experiences and identities – realities that would seem more complex than Sennett's analysis suggests. Aspects of Sennett's arguments may have relevance, however, as there are disturbing indications that such commitments cannot be taken for granted for the future. Current policies may be effectively undermining precisely the qualities that have such relevance for the public service professionals' development role, just as they may be undermining government agendas to strengthen social capital, enhancing relationships of trust, mutual responsibility and commitment.

Looking backwards/looking forwards: is a tipping point being reached?

Labour's policies for public service modernisation face both ways, it has been asserted, rather than offering a coherent 'third way' (Newman and Vidler, 2006). This Janus-like quality emerges from our research in a number of ways. There were, for example, aspects of modernisation that were actively welcomed by a number of our respondents. These professionals identified with the aims of decentralisation and enhanced coordination at the neighbourhood level, welcoming these as opportunities for improving service delivery – closing the gaps between service provision in the most deprived areas and elsewhere, pursuing the social justice agendas of the 'new professionalism'.

The majority took a somewhat different view, however, pointing to the re-assertion of centralisation and the diminishing scope for the exercise of precisely those aspects of their professional role that were most central to the development function. Far from promoting capacity building and active citizenship, such policies were undermining relationships of cooperation and trust, promoting more individualised forms of competition – effectively 'taking the community out of the voluntary and community sector' in the pursuit of the new managerialism. This is suggestive of de-professionalisation, just as it is suggestive of continuity with the neoliberal agendas of preceding governments, with few, if any, indications of innovation in pursuit of social democratic forms of social solidarity.

As we have argued in previous chapters, a psycho-social approach can provide valuable insights into professionals' complex and varying responses to the challenges of public service modernisation. Professional identities, motivations and values are rooted in individuals' personal biographies, and develop as professionals reflect on their changing experiences over time. These identities, motivations and values seem to have been more durable than Sennett's study might have predicted. But here too, a Janus-like quality emerges from our research. Looking forwards to the next generation of public service professionals there would seem to be a number of grounds for concern. Professional identities, motivations and values are being shaped in very different contexts, within the framework of current policy agendas. How might this impact on the ways in which the next generations of public service professionals navigate the contradictions of public service modernisation? Has community engagement and youth work reached a tipping point?

International parallels

There would also seem to be parallels when it comes to the challenges facing those concerned with international development work. Debates about de-professionalisation have similar, if not even greater relevance, for example. INGOs and NGOs have both criticised and themselves been criticised for promoting the use of para professionals such as para professional teachers, for instance. Para professionals have provided the only realistic answer to desperate shortages of trained teachers and/or the resources to pay teachers' salaries in too many contexts. And para professional teaching roles open up employment opportunities for local people. Yet the use of para teachers has been resisted too – on the grounds that this undermines the case for employing adequately trained teachers in the first place.

This is but one example of the tensions and contradictions that are inherent in the current policy context, internationally as well as more locally, within Britain. Do current policies threaten a 'new tyranny', as Cooke and Kothari (2001) have suggested, for example, or do they offer the potential for developing new approaches to social transformation (Hickey and Mohan, 2004)? These debates also have increasing relevance for those concerned with the future of professionals and professionalism in Britain, as the following and concluding chapter will argue in more detail, as the interconnections between the local and the global become more clearly evident, in the context of increasing globalisation.

TEN

The future of development work

Reflecting on 'Writing in and against time', Back challenges the idea 'that we can write about societies as if they hold still while we sketch them. What anthropologists call the "ethnographic present" (ie the idea that eternal assertions can be made like "Nuer religion is ..." or "middle-class culture is ...") simply seems absurd when you think about it', Back continues (2004, p 204). 'The idea that we are writing in time, at a particular moment, which is partial and positioned and in place, is a major advance', he suggests. 'I think we are also writing against time, trying to capture an outline of an existence that is fleeting', Back concludes (2004, p 204), while re-affirming his personal commitment to doing precisely this, listening and speaking to people who 'live the consequence of the globalised world' with respect and humility 'while maintaining critical judgement' (2004, p 213).

This concluding chapter starts from here, recognising the challenges involved in attempting to capture the dilemmas of the current context, let alone attempting to project future scenarios for development workers in the years to come. The pace of change has, in recent years, been particularly rapid in public policy terms, with no immediate prospect of any slowing down. Communities seeking to engage with planners and service providers face a potentially bewildering array of structures, marked by increasing complexity and growing fragmentation. As a result, the need for development work would seem likely to continue, if not increase. While our focus will be predominantly British, there is some evidence to suggest that similar tendencies may be identified more widely.

Meanwhile, communities have become increasingly diverse, it has been argued, and identities perceived as increasingly complex, in their turn (Hall, 1991; Bhabha, 1994; Solomos, 2003). The chapter moves on to summarise the arguments in support of this view. Globalisation has been associated with changing patterns of migration and population churn, changes that have been debated from varying perspectives along the political spectrum. Despite certain popular expressions of nostalgia for some (mythically) homogeneous British or English past, the phenomena of continuing population churn, with diasporic communities and hybrid identities, would seem more likely to be here to stay. Once again, there would seem to be significant implications for development work. If established communities find governance structures confusing, these challenges tend to be compounded for newer arrivals. Engaging and empowering newer communities – without exacerbating tensions within and between these newer arrivals and more established communities – represent major challenges for development workers charged with the promotion of community cohesion and social solidarity. Here too, then, the need for development work would seem likely to continue, if not to increase, both in volume and complexity.

Having summarised the continuing case for development work, the second section of this chapter focuses on the implications for development workers of these increasingly complex and challenging scenarios. On the basis of the evidence from previous chapters, what can we learn about the values, motivations and personal qualities workers need to cope with this complexity? What might be the implications for the education, training, support and continuing professional development of development workers? And what might be the implications for public policies, including public policies for community development and community engagement in structures of governance?

Increasing complexity and growing fragmentation

As previous chapters have already suggested, public service modernisation has been promoted within the context of wider strategies – to reconfigure relationships between civil society, the market and the state. Neoliberal economic policies have been accompanied by initiatives to increase user choice, also emphasising the importance of the voice of individuals as consumers within the public service sector. Development workers have been tasked with managing the competing pressures that arise as a result, attempting to balance agendas for individual consumer voice and choice with the tensions inherent in balancing these with agendas for inclusion and social justice.

Looking forward, there seems no particular reason to suppose that these pressures are likely to decrease in the immediate future; on the contrary, in fact. In Britain, the modernisation of public services has been continuing apace, with proposals for further fragmentation in the education system through accelerating the development of academy schools, for example. New coordination mechanisms such as the National Community Empowerment Partnership are developing in tandem, as agencies struggle to keep pace with changes, such as the new initiatives to improve the quality, coordination and evidence of community empowerment across England. As it is, publicly funded bodies with structures that aim to engage service users and communities include local strategic partnerships, along with local thematic groups such as crime reduction partnerships, neighbourhood and ward forums, a variety of health structures including the new local involvement networks, registered social landlords and school governing bodies in both local authority and academy sectors.

Reflecting on the challenges posed by these differing structures for community engagement, local residents have been raising the difficulties of knowing where to go, when they want to make their voices heard, as a recent study has identified (Blake et al, 2008). One of Blake's respondents noted, "There is a chronic and severe lack of information on how to engage. The problem is that we don't have a map of the decision-makers" (quoted in Blake et al, 2008), highlighting the importance of local development workers providing assistance in navigating through this complex and rapidly shifting terrain. This was daunting enough for established communities, this particular study concluded, let alone for newer arrivals, in the wider context of super-diversity and rapid population churn.

While much of the focus in this book has been on the challenges posed for development workers as a result of increasing complexity and the growing fragmentation of services in Britain, there would also seem to be wider resonances. In India, for example, Panchayati Raj structures of local governance provide spaces for community engagement, spaces that have been opened up, following constitutional amendments in the 1990s, to promote more effective representation for women and for disadvantaged groups, scheduled tribes and castes. While these efforts to encourage more inclusive forms of participation have been developed, however, other structures have been addressing a range of key issues locally, issues such as education, water and environmental pollution. The operation of these structures has been described in terms of wider strategies to promote liberalisation, part of economic reforms that entail new relationships between the state and the citizen, relationships in which those with the most resources and power may exert the greatest influence, with the loudest voices. Even if less advantaged groups succeed in making their voices heard in the Panchayati Raj structures, it has been suggested, key decisions about essential services may actually be being taken elsewhere (Reddy, 2002) – decisions about water provision being taken to maximise land owners' profits through irrigating their crops, for example, rather than taking sufficient account of the needs of less advantaged groups, such as their need for water for their animals and for washing. Here too, then, increasing complexity and fragmentation have been accompanying the neoliberal strategies that have been changing relationships between civil society, the state and the market. Without support from development workers, less advantaged groups have correspondingly reduced prospects of making their voices effectively heard, whatever the formal arrangements for community participation and empowerment.

Increasing diversity and population churn

Meanwhile, it has been suggested, communities themselves are becoming more diverse. There is a long established literature, exploring the complex interconnections between processes of capitalist globalisation, population migrations and social and cultural change. As Smith was arguing much earlier, 'We are constantly being reminded that the globe we inhabit is becoming smaller and more integrated. In short our world has become a single place' (Smith, 1995, p 1). Yet, he went on to point out, 'we are witnessing a rebirth of ethnic nationalism, or religious fundamentalisms and of group antagonisms which were thought to have been long buried' (Smith, 1995, pp 1-3), and this was before the attack on the twin towers in New York and the so-called 'War on Terror'. Since then, capitalist globalisation has been associated with even sharper tensions and increasing anxieties. 'Community cohesion' has become a major challenge, however this is defined, whether framed within the context of strategies to replace multiculturalism with policies to promote the social and cultural assimilation of minority communities or whether framed within the context of strategies to promote social solidarity, based on respect for diversity and cultural difference.

People continue to move, within and between states, whether to escape the effects of war, famine, flood, drought, ethnic, religious or political persecution or whether to seek new opportunities for education and employment – or some combination of the above. Forced displacements, as measured by UNHCR (United Nations High Commissioner for Refugees) statistics on refugee and asylum trends, have begun to rise again, following falls in recent years, reaching some 10 million in 2007. Unsurprisingly, given the impact of the so-called War on Terror, and the violence that followed the invasion of Iraq, Iraqis topped the asylum statistics in 2006 (although the trend began to fall, subsequently). While industrialised nations have been receiving fewer applications for asylum (even if this is not the impression that might emerge from reading the tabloid press on occasion), there have been increases in the numbers of internally displaced people, with an estimated 24.5 million, in 2007, civilians, mostly women and children, forced to flee within the borders of their own countries because of conflict or persecution, together with those forced to move as a result of natural disasters or because of development projects such as the construction of major dams. Population churn is so clearly both an international and a more local phenomenon, both in terms of the causes and in terms of the effects – although not necessarily in the ways that may be feared by xenophobes, arguing for further restrictions on asylum seekers in industrialised nations.

Meanwhile, migration in search of education and employment opportunities continues to feature significantly, both in Britain and beyond. Britain has a long and chequered history, with public policy responses that have been described as 'Janus-faced', developing an increasingly restrictive stance towards immigration, while attempting to balance this with community-based initiatives from 'race' relations policies to the present community cohesion policies (Craig, 2007). Despite some progressive initiatives, it has been argued, the racism inherent in policy and practice continues (Craig, 2007), although it is important not to exaggerate the barriers to community cohesion, overall. As the Commission on Integration and Cohesion has pointed out, over 80% of those who responded to the Citizenship Survey in 2007 agreed with the view that their local area was a place where people from different backgrounds got on well together (COIC, 2007).

The most recent waves of migration to Britain have been estimated as including three quarters of a million migrants from the EU accession states, estimates that are almost certainly understated. Research has demonstrated that, far from benefiting from unfair advantages, as myths and stereotypes appearing in the tabloid press have suggested, these migrants have experienced particular disadvantages, being disproportionately likely to be in low-skilled and low-paid jobs (whatever their actual qualifications), living in poor housing conditions and lacking effective access to services (Markova and Black, 2007; Spencer et al, 2007). This is a situation that poses major challenges for policy and practice, including community development practice.

New arrivals typically need community development support as a matter of urgency. Too often they lack the most basic information about how to access services, information and advice that can be provided if development workers are tasked with making contact, working through informal community networks as well as working through more formal structures, including anchor organisations and faith-based groups. Such outreach support needs to be provided in ways that promote cohesion rather than exacerbating competition for scarce resources within and between communities, including established minority communities.

Recent research has identified a range of examples of promising practices, ways in which newcomers *are* being reached effectively, building solidarity rather than increasing tensions within and between communities (Blake et al, 2008). As this research report concludes, however, these promising practices in turn depend on the development and implementation of community development strategies, resourced to engage with new arrivals as well as with established communities, providing outreach support, working with anchor organisations to organise shared community events and initiatives and to facilitate community advocacy and campaigning, including campaigning to challenge racism and other forms of discrimination and oppression. Diversity and population change seem likely to be continuing features of life in Britain and beyond, and so does the need for development work to promote social solidarity and social justice.

Reflecting on this, Putnam has concluded that, 'One of the most important challenges facing modern societies, and at the same time, one of the most significant opportunities, is the increase in ethnic and social heterogeneity in virtually all advanced countries. The most certain prediction that we can make about almost any modern society is that it will be more diverse a generation from now than it is today' (Putnam, 2007, p 137). This he considered as a major challenge, in terms of the impact on social capital. On the basis of evidence from the US, Putnam argued, ethnically diverse neighbourhoods seemed to be associated with lower levels of social trust. People were more likely to retreat into their own comfort zones – a process that he described as 'hunkering down'. Alternative and more socially inclusive outcomes were possible, however: there were examples of trust developing over time. Further research was needed, he concluded, in order to develop more systematic understandings of how this might be facilitated, how to build bridges between diverse communities, not by trying to make 'them like us' but rather 'by creating a new, more capacious sense of "we", a reconstruction of diversity that does not bleach out ethnic specificities, but creates overarching identities that ensure that those specificities do not trigger the allergic, "hunker down" reaction' (Putnam, 2007, pp 163-4). Whatever reservations might have been expressed about his concept of social capital in theory (Fine, 2001), Putnam's conclusions have potential resonance for professional practice here – for the development worker's role, facilitating the development of social solidarity within and between diverse communities.

Increasing global challenges

Meanwhile, the context for development work is not only being complicated by increasing diversity and population churn. Inequalities have also been increasing. The contemporary context has been described in terms of the paradox: the 'polarization of opulence and deprivation', both within and between countries internationally (Greig et al, 2007, p 4). The richest 20% of the world's population accounted for 70% of income in 1960. By 1991 this share had increased to 85% while the bottom 20%'s share declined from 2.3% to 1.4%. The principal polarity, it has been argued, 'is not between rich and poor countries, but between rich and poor people across the globe' (Rapley, 2004, p 88, quoted in Greig et al, 2007, p 4). Neoliberal economic strategies have been associated with rapid economic growth in specific contexts, but far from trickling down to benefit the poorest, the benefits of economic growth have been associated with increasing polarisation, with phenomenal gaps between the richest and the poorest. India and China provide illustrations here.

As George and Wilding have pointed out, increasing globalisation does not necessarily imply increasing inequalities (George and Wilding, 2002). But neoliberal globalisation has to be challenged, with structural economic changes at international level if poverty is to be effectively tackled. 'Neo-liberal ideology is not necessary', they conclude, in the sense that the neoliberal forms of globalisation that have dominated in recent decades 'do not simply have to be accepted as inevitable' (George and Wilding, 2002, p 174). As activists at World Social Forums have been arguing, 'another world is possible', which is not in any way to underestimate the challenges that are involved in attempting to build alternative futures. The point to emphasise here is simply this: that development workers need to have a critical understanding of the underlying causes of increasing inequalities if they are to work effectively with those most directly affected.

As previous chapters have already argued, neoliberal ideologies have also been centrally important, in terms of their impact on welfare, persuading governments to cut back on the provision of public services to meet increasing social needs. In Britain, recent years have been characterised by what Alcock and Craig have described as 'the New Welfare Mix', a new and more eclectic mix of public, voluntary and increasingly private provision (Alcock and Craig, 2001). These changes have fundamentally altered the very nature of many public services, in their view, and 'are unlikely to be reversed in the foreseeable future' (Alcock and Craig, 2001, p 136). In Britain, as in so many contexts then, these changes can be expected to pose continuing problems for development workers, faced with increasing fragmentation and complexity in the provision of services for the communities that they are attempting to serve.

Meanwhile, internationally, it has been argued, some of the optimism that accompanied the spread of democracy and rights-based approaches to development was already beginning to ebb by the end of the 1990s (Cornwall and Molyneux, 2008). Although rights-based approaches have been associated with increasing legitimacy for the pursuit of social justice agendas – 'providing a more authoritative basis for advocacy', in the words of the former president of Ireland and international rights activist, Mary Robinson – reservations have been expressed as to how far rights are actually being realised in practice, including reservations as to the implications for women's rights. Governments tend to be selective in their promotion of rights, it has been argued, and, as Cornwall and Molyneux have also pointed out, in the context of neoliberal globalisation, 'sceptics question the "right to exploit" awarded to many transnational companies (TNCs) in developing countries' (Cornwall and Molyneux, 2008, p 5). Here too, there are continuing challenges and dilemmas for development workers committed to supporting individuals and communities in realising their rights for social, economic, political and cultural rights together with their rights to environmental justice in a world in which the consequences of unsustainable forms of development are disproportionately borne by the poorest and most vulnerable. Inclusive citizenship requires justice, Kabeer has argued, together with recognition, self-determination and solidarity (Kabeer, 2005), thereby summarising agendas for development workers for years to come.

Distinctive values, motivations and personal qualities needed for development work

Following the recent death of a much respected youth and community worker, in a tragic cycling accident, a memorial meeting was held to celebrate his life and work. The tributes from former colleagues, community activists and young people whose lives he had touched provided moving accounts of what it was about this young man that had made such a difference to so many lives. The fact that he always had time for people was a recurring theme. He was a person who listened to others with respect and he was there for people, building relationships of trust consistently over time. He was enthusiastic, fun-loving and most importantly, he was affirmative, giving young people the confidence to aim further, just as he himself had gained confidence from the encouragement shown to him, as a young person growing up in an area where expectations of young people were generally limited. Much the same could be said of Jeremy Brent, one of the participants in our research who died suddenly not long after we had completed it. Several of Jeremy's insights and experiences can be found in this book. From 1975 Jeremy worked on a Bristol housing estate, first for an adventure playground, then in and around, and running, the youth centre. As John Westcott put it in the booklet produced for Jeremy's Memorial Day on 2 September 2006, 'no one had ever worked at Southmead for so long ... it turned out to be his life work'. As Jeremy himself put it, with typical honesty about his ambivalences:

> 'This quarter of a century's involvement with Southmead puzzles me. It was not my intention to stay so long when I first took work there on a six-month contract. Staying that long does indicate a strong attachment – to ... something. This something has not always been Southmead itself, with which I have a love/hate relationship, but the continual feeling I have of unfinished business with the place and the people, like a familial relationship.'

In another dedication to Jeremy, Professor Richard Johnson added, "his working life, for reasons he admitted finding 'puzzling', was certainly focused on helping young people to find some agency of their own, but it was also, in itself, a model or example of social solidarity, and of the recognition of our need for help, and our need to give it, of, in short, our social dependency, that was lived through to the end". It is both with great pride and considerable humility that we have dedicated this book to Jeremy, who exemplified what Johnson described as that 'sustained human solidarity' which is so central to effective development work.

Both of the individuals whose deaths we have just reflected on help remind us of one of the key themes of this book, that is, the relationship between ethical principles and personal qualities. It will be remembered that in Chapter One we described two different approaches to ethics: an 'impartialist' approach concerned with abstract principles, and a partialist or situational approach concerned with context, relationships and human specificity. We suggested that principles were vital for development work but in and of themselves they were insufficient. We hope that by now our argument will have become clearer.

Development work occurs on a social terrain that is more contested, ambiguous and subject to flux and change than possibly any other location. Following Bonnie Honig (1996), we call this 'dilemmatic space'. Without principles to provide some kind of guidance the development worker will soon become lost, and without an ethical compass to move about, the dangers of opportunism and pragmatism will quickly loom. But the problem is that in today's world principles are not enough. What happens when two cherished principles, such as equality and liberty, clash? How does a commitment to social justice help the worker when it is not at all clear what, according to this principle, is the right thing to do in a situation, for example, where different groups have conflicting concepts of fairness? In this book, via both short vignettes and long case studies, we have tried to illustrate how these kinds of ambiguous and uncertain situations constantly recur in the working lives of development workers. To act ethically in such situations we have argued that the development worker must bring to the job a set of human qualities alongside their principles. These qualities we have referred to as 'capacities'. A capacity draws attention to something that exists as a potentiality of an individual or group. We use this concept in preference both to Nussbaum's more finite concept of 'capability' and particularly as an alternative to narrow and mechanistic concepts of measurable 'competences' which somehow or another can be ticked off against a checklist of essential attributes a development worker should have. As a potentiality a capacity represents a latent power or resource that the person can draw on. In this book we have outlined a number of capacities that we regard as crucial to the role of the development worker. These include the capacity:

- to contain uncertainty, ambiguity and complexity without resort to simplistic splitting into good/bad, black/white, us/them, and so on;
- for self-authorisation, that is, the capacity to find the courage to act in situations where there is no obvious right thing to do;
- for reflexivity, that is, to take oneself as an object of inquiry and curiosity and hence to be able to suspend belief about oneself; all this as a way of sustaining a critical approach to oneself, one's values and beliefs, one's strengths and weaknesses, the nature of one's power and authority, and so on;
- to contain emotions such as anger, resentment, hope and cynicism without suppressing them and hence to be both passionate and thoughtful.

These capacities resemble human qualities or virtues that we believe are necessary if the development worker is to operate in a principled way in dilemmatic space. But of course the development worker is not an island and we see these capacities as much as a property of the network or group as of the individual. And for this to be the case the group itself must be one that encourages dialogue, one where different perspectives are welcomed, where constructive criticism can be given and received and so on.

Previous chapters have also explored the motivations and values that development workers bring to the role. Our research provided evidence of the continuing significance of formative experiences, the personal, social and political influences that contributed to the formation of workers' principles and had constituted their 'habitus'. While these formative experiences varied, just as reactions to experiences varied, common threads have emerged. Whatever their differences in terms of class background, 'race' and gender, and their differing experiences, the participants in our research study seemed to share some common commitments, a 'burning desire' (Moon, 2005, p 9) even, to 'making a difference'. For them, the development role represented 'so much more than a job'. As previous chapters have also illustrated, however, the meanings attached to 'making a difference' seemed less than precise.

Development workers expressed some considerable anxieties for the future, however, as the previous chapter has also suggested. While newer entrants to the profession still had commitment, in the view of some of the more experienced professionals, the next generation tended to be more career-orientated and there was a risk of losing sight of the wider goals but focusing on delivering outputs to the detriment of initiative and creativity in the pursuit of social justice agendas. Was a tipping point being reached? Professional identities, motivations and values had proved relatively resilient so far, but that in no way guaranteed that the future direction of travel would be towards a 'new professionalism' rather than towards processes of de-professionalisation. There did seem to be broad agreement, however, that, in whichever direction, change seemed likely to be the only constant. Individual identities, motivations and values could be expected to shift, as new generations of professionals emerge with differing formations and 'habitus'. As the previous section of this chapter has already argued, these new generations of professionals can be expected to face continuing change, working in contexts of increasing complexity, locally, as well as being affected by increasing global challenges.

In response to these processes of change, development workers can also be expected to face increasing dilemmas, new situations in which professional ethical codes can provide no more than the most approximate guides to action (if, indeed, they ever could). They will be required to exercise professional judgement, balancing the need to hold on to professional identities and values while reacting flexibly to changing circumstances and emerging needs, as reflexive practitioners. And they will need advanced levels of knowledge, skills and critical understanding, in order to analyse the scope for strategic responses, as well as having the skills to enable communities to develop strategic responses for themselves.

Implications for the education and continuing professional development of development workers

The importance of professional education and training has already emerged from previous chapters. So has the importance of continuing professional development, backed by non-managerial supervision, to provide safe spaces to facilitate ongoing cycles of reflection and action. Development workers need to become new types of professionals, it has been suggested, self-reflexive professionals with the capacity to bridge the gap between theory and practice, professional practitioners who are also researchers as well as activists.

This in turn implies new roles for the universities and colleges that provide education, training and continuing professional development. Looking outwards, they could be providing precisely such safe spaces. As Lyn Tett has argued, with specific reference to community education, 'it is all too easy to lose our vision of ourselves as a profession that is about challenging existing inequalities when much of the policy discourse is about incorporating communities into existing structures and silencing their disseminating views'. She went on to suggest, however, that 'The university sector has a role to play in articulating this [ie more progressive] vision both through our initial professional education course and through continuing professional development that provides opportunities to stimulate debate and share a vision of what might be possible across our field' (Tett, 2008, pp 27-8). 'We need to think collectively', she continued, 'about how we can provide spaces for practitioners to come together to debate, share problems and build alliances so that we have a clearer view of where we stand and what we stand for. This would give us the possibility of ... "reclaiming a notion of professionalism" that "includes the capacity to express and contest professional and political purpose, not just to act as State functionaries"' (Tett, 2008, p 28).

Workshops and seminars can offer opportunities for reflection, sharing knowledge and skills, co-producing new knowledge and jointly exploring the implications of research findings. Service users and communities can, and do, contribute to professional education and training, just as professionals can and do participate in research. There is an emerging body of knowledge and critical analysis about ways of promoting teaching and learning, including the potential role of higher education institutions themselves as agents of development and social change (Taylor and Fransman, 2003).

In Britain, however, powerful pressures are currently driving in opposite directions. Like the rest of the public service sector, higher education is under considerable pressure for increasing marketisation, including pressures to work more closely to employers' agendas to meet the skills requirements for competitiveness in the global economy. Higher education, it has been argued, should be potentially more profit-led rather than values-led and 'increasingly employer-led, more responsive to the needs of large employers and be subject to more employer-led funding' (Maclachlan, 2008, p 18). In Maclachlan's view, 'it becomes clear that the spaces for critical, challenging counter hegemonic teaching, learning and research that are part of what a university should be all about, are becoming increasingly and alarmingly diminished' (Maclachlan, 2008, p 19). Narrowly conceived, then, such agendas risk stifling precisely the qualities required for the development of the 'new professionalism', learning and teaching to promote reflexivity, creativity and critical thinking. The development of such alternatives is beyond the scope of this particular book. The point is simply to signal the importance of doing precisely this, in partnership with professionals and their organisations and trade unions, alongside colleagues within the higher education sector itself.

Implications for public policy

This book has focused on development workers and their dilemmas and challenges rather than focusing on public policy per se. Rather than launching into our own suggestions for public policy reform at this point, we would like to conclude by focusing on the contributions that development workers themselves might make to debates on the development of public policies. As this chapter has already argued, the future does not have to be perceived as immutably fixed – increasing globalisation does not necessarily imply increasing inequalities (George and Wilding, 2002). As George and Wilding have pointed out, the neoliberal forms of globalisation that have dominated in recent decades 'do not simply have to be accepted as inevitable' (George and Wilding, 2002, p 174). Another world is possible.

Development workers need the knowledge and critical understanding to identify the scope for alternative approaches locally, linking with wider coalitions campaigning for policy changes at national and international levels too. And they need the personal qualities that will enable them to work effectively with diverse communities, building solidarity within and between communities, constructing partnerships between communities and their potential allies, contributing to the creation of sustainable coalitions for progressive social change.

References

Abel-Smith, B. and Townsend, P. (1965) *The Poor and the Poorest*, London, Bell and Sons.

Alcock, P. (2006) *Understanding Poverty* (3rd edn), Basingstoke: Palgrave.

Alcock, P. and Craig, G. (eds) (2001) 'The United Kingdom: rolling back the state?', in P. Alcock and G. Craig (eds) *International Social Policy*, Basingstoke: Palgrave, pp 124-42.

Alford, C.F. (1992) *Group Psychology and Political Theory*, London/New Haven, CT: Yale University Press.

Anastacio, J., Gidley, B., Hart, L., Keith, M., Kowarzik, U. and Mayo, M. (2000) *Reflecting Realities: Participants' Perspectives on Integrated Communities and Sustainable Development*, Bristol: The Policy Press.

Anderson, R. (ed) (1992) *Clinical Lecture on Klein & Bion*, London: Tavistock/Routledge.

Back, L. (2004) 'Writing in and against time', in M. Bulmer and J. Solomos (eds) *Researching Race and Racism*, London: Routledge, pp 203-13.

Bailey, D. and Schwartzberg, S. (1995) *Ethical and Legal Dilemmas in Occupational Therapy*, Philadelphia, PA: Davis.

Balloch, S. and Taylor, M. (eds) (2001) *Partnership Working*, Bristol: The Policy Press.

Banks, S. (1995) *Ethics and Values in Social Work*, London: Macmillan.

Banks, S. (ed) (1999) *Ethical Issues in Youth Work*, London: Routledge.

Banks, S. (2004) *Ethics, Accountability and the Social Professions*, Basingstoke: Palgrave Macmillan.

Banks, S. (2006) *Ethics and Values in Social Work* (3rd edn), Basingstoke: Palgrave.

Banks, S. and Orten, A. (2005) '"The grit in the oyster": community development workers in a modernizing local authority', *Community Development Journal*, vol 42, no 1, pp 97-113.

Banks, S. and Williams, R. (2005) 'Accounting for ethical difficulties in social welfare work: issues, problems and dilemmas', *British Journal of Social Work*, vol 35, no 7, pp 1005-22.

Banks, S., Butcher, H. and Robertson, J. (2003) *Managing Community Practice*, Bristol: The Policy Press.

Barber, B. (1984) *Strong Democracy: Participatory Politics for a New Age*, Berkeley, CA: University of California Press.

Barnes, M. (2006) 'Whose spaces? Contestations and negotiations in health and community regeneration forums in England', in A. Cornwall and V.S. Coelho (eds) *Spaces for Change? The Politics of Citizen Participation in New Democratic Arenas*, London: Zed Books.

Barr, M. (2005) 'A curriculum by any other name … The parallels between youth work and criminal justice', *Youth and Policy*, vol 86, pp 19-32.

Bateson, G. (1972) *Steps to an Ecology of Mind: Collected Essays in Anthropology, Psychiatry, Evolution, and Epistemology*, Chicago, IL: University Of Chicago Press.

Bauman, Z. (1993) *Postmodern Ethics*, Cambridge: Polity Press.

Beck, U. (1992) *Risk Society: Towards a New Modernity*, London: Sage Publications.

Beck, U. (1997) *The Reinvention of Politics: Rethinking Modernity in the Global Social Order*, Cambridge: Polity Press.

Benjamin, J. (1978) 'Authority and the family revisited: or, a world without fathers?', *New German Critique*, pp 35-57.

Benjamin, J. (1990) *Psychoanalysis, Feminism and the Problem of Domination*, London: Virago.

Benjamin, J. (2004) 'Beyond doer and done to: an intersubjective view of thirdness', *Psychoanalytic Quarterly*, vol LXXIII, pp 5-46.

Bhabha, H. (1994) *The Location of Culture*, London: Routledge.

Bion, W. (1962) *Learning from Experience*, London: Heinemann.

Blake, G., Diamond, J., Foot, J., Gidley, B., Mayo, M., Shukra, K. and Yarnit, M. (2008) *Community Engagement and Community Cohesion*, York: Joseph Rowntree Foundation.

Bottery, M. (1998) *Professionals and Policy*, London: Cassell.

Bourdieu, P. (1977) *Outline of a Theory of Practice* (trans R. Nice), Cambridge: Cambridge University Press.

Bourdieu, P. (1999) *The Weight of the World: Social Suffering in Contemporary Society*, Cambridge: Polity Press.

Brent, J. (1997) 'Community without unity', in P. Hoggett (ed) *Contested Communities: Experiences, Struggles, Policies*, Bristol: The Policy Press.

Briner, R., Poppleton, M., Owens, S. and Kiefer, T. (2007) *The Nature, Causes and Consequences of Harm in Emotionally Demanding Occupations*, London: Health and Safety Executive (www.hse.gov.uk/research/rrhtm/rr610.htm).

Brown, G., Harris, T. and Bifulco, A. (1986) 'Long term effects of early loss of parent', in M. Rutter, C. Izard and P. Read (eds) *Depression in Young People: Developmental and Clinical Perspectives*, New York: Guilford Press.

Burrows, R. and Loader, B. (1994) *Towards a Post-Fordist Welfare State?*, London: Routledge.

Cain, H. and Yuval-Davis, N. (1990) 'The equal opportunities community and the anti-racist struggle', *Critical Social Policy*, vol 29, pp 5-26.

Cantle Report (2001) *Community Cohesion: A Report of the Review Team*, London: Community Cohesion Review Team, Home Office.

Caplan, R. (1994) 'Stress, anxiety and depression in hospital consultants, general practitioners and senior health care managers', *British Medical Journal*, vol 309, pp 1261-3.

Carr, W. (2001) 'The exercise of authority in a dependent context', in L. Gould, L. Stapley and M. Stein (eds) *The Systems Psychodynamics of Organisations*, London: Karnac.

Carter, C. (1979) *Authority and Democracy*, London: Routledge and Kegan Paul.

Causer, G. and Exworthy, M. (1999) 'Professionals as managers across the public sector', in M. Exworthy and S. Halford (eds) *Professionals and the New Managerialism in the Public Sector*, Buckingham: Open University Press.

CDP Inter-Project Editorial Team (1977) *The Costs of Industrial Change*, London, CDP Inter-Project Editorial Team.

Chapman, J. (2003) 'Hatred and corruption of task', *Organisational and Social Dynamics*, vol 3, no 1, pp 40-60.

Clark, D., Fox, J. and Treakle, K. (eds) (2003) *Demanding Accountability: Civil Society Claims and the World Bank Inspection Panel*, Lanham, MD: Oxford: Rowman and Littlefield.

Clarke, J., Gewirtz, S. and McLaughlin, E. (eds) (2000) *New Managerialism, New Welfare?*, London: Sage Publications.

Clarke, J., Smith, N. and Vidler, E. (2006) 'The indeterminacy of choice: political and organisational implications', *Social Policy and Society*, vol 5, no 3, pp 327-36.

Coates, K. and Silburn, R. (1970) *Poverty: The Forgotten Englishmen*, London: Penguin.

Cockburn, C. (1977) *The Local State: Management of Cities and People*, London: Pluto Press.

COIC (Commission on Integration and Cohesion) (2007) *Our Shared Future*, Report of the Commission on Integration and Cohesion, (www.integrationandcohesion.org.uk).

Compass (2006) *The Good Society: Compass Programme for Renewal*, London: Compass and Lawrence & Wishart.

Cooke, B. and Kothari, U. (eds) (2001) *Participation: The New Tyranny?*, London: Zed Books.

Cooper, A. and Lousada, J. (2005) *Borderline Welfare: Feeling and Fear of Feeling in Modern Welfare*, London: Karnac.

Cooper, C. and Kelly, M. (1993) 'Occupational stress in headteachers: a national UK study', *Journal of Educational Psychology*, vol 63, pp 130-43.

Cornwall, A. (2008) 'Unpacking "participation": Models, meanings and practices', *Community Development Journal*, vol 43, no 3, pp 269-83.

Cornwall, A. and Molyneux, M. (2008) 'The politics of rights – dilemmas for feminist praxis', in A. Cornwall and M. Molyneux (eds) *The Politics of Rights*, London: Routledge.

Craig, G. (2007) '"Cunning, unprincipled, loathsome": the racist tail wags the welfare dog', *Journal of Social Policy*, vol 36, pp 605-23.

Craig, G., Derricourt, N. and Loney, M. (eds) (1982) *Community Work and the State*, London: Routledge and Kegan Paul.

Curno, P. (ed) (1978) *Political Issues and Community Work*, London, Routledge and Kegan Paul.

Dahl, R. (1961) *Who Governs?*, New Haven, CT: Yale University Press.

Dahl, R. (1967) *Pluralist Democracy in the United States: Conflict and Consent*, New York: Rand MacNally.

Davies, B. (2005) 'If youth matters, where is the youth work?', *Youth and Policy*, vol 89, pp 21-6.

Dawkins, R. (1976) *The Selfish Gene*, Oxford: Oxford University Press.

Deacon, A. and Mann, K. (1999) 'Agency, modernity and social policy', *Journal of Social Policy*, vol 28, no 3, pp 413-35.

DES (Department for Education and Skills) (2005) *Youth Matters*, Green Paper, London: DES/The Stationery Office.

DES (2006) *Youth Matters: Next Steps*, London: DES/The Stationery Office.

DH (Department of Health) (2000) *The NHS Plan: A Plan for Investment, A Plan for Reform*, London: DH.

Dominelli, L. (1990) *Women and Community Action*, Birmingham, Venture Press.

Downton, J. and Wehr, P. (1997) *The Persistent Activist: How Peace Careers Develop and Survive*, Boulder, CO: Westview Press.

Du Gay, P. (2000) *In Praise of Bureaucracy: Weber/Organisation/Ethics*, London: Sage Publications.

Durkin, L. and Douieb, B. (1975) 'The mental patients' union', in D. Jones and M. Mayo (eds) *Community Work Two*, London: Routledge and Kegan Paul, pp 177-91.

East London Claimants Union (1973) 'East London Claimants Union and the concept of self-management', in D. Jones and M. Mayo (eds) *Community Work On*, London: Routledge and Kegan Paul, pp 79-89.

Etzioni, A. (1961) *A Comparative Analysis of Complex Organisations*, Glencoe, IL: Free Press.

Exworthy, M. and Halford, S. (1999) *Professionals and the New Managerialism in the Public Sector*, Buckingham: Open University Press.

Farnsworth, K. and Holden, C. (2006) 'The business–social policy nexus: corporate power and corporate inputs into social policy', *Journal of Social Policy*, vol 35, no 3, pp 473-94.

Ferguson, H. (2004) *Protecting Children in Time*, Basingstoke: Palgrave Macmillan.

Fine, B. (2001) *Social Capital Versus Social Theory*, London: Routledge.

Fiorini, A. (2000) *The Third Force: The Rise of Transnational Civil Society*, Washington, DC: Carnegie Endowment for International Peace.

Fitzpatrick, S. and Jones, A. (2005) 'Pursuing social justice or social cohesion?: coercion in street homelessness policies in England', *Journal of Social Policy*, vol 34, no 3, pp 389-406.

Fitzpatrick, T. (2005) *New Theories of Welfare*, Basingstoke: Palgrave.

Fitzsimons, A. (2007) 'Working with the contradictions – New Labour's social exclusion policies', *Youth and Policy*, vol 94, pp 51-9.

Flathman, R.E. (1990) 'Concepts in social and political philosophy', Basingstoke: Macmillan (reprinted in J. Raz [ed] *Authority*, London: Basil Blackwell).

Foucault, M. (1977) *Discipline and Punish: The Rise of the Prison*, Harmondsworth: Penguin.

Foucault, M. (1980) *Power/Knowledge*, Brighton: Harvester.

Fraser, N. (1995) 'From redistribution to recognition? Dilemmas of justice in a "postsocialist" age', *New Left Review*, vol 212, pp 68-93.

Freeman, J. (1970) *The Tyranny of Structurelessness*, USA Women's Liberation Movement pamphlet.

Freidson, E. (2001) *Professionalism*, Chicago, IL: University of Chicago Press.

Freire, P. (1972) *Pedagogy of the Oppressed*, Harmondsworth: Penguin Books.

Freire, P. (1995) *Paulo Freire at the Institute*, London: Institute of Education.

French, J. Jr and Raven, B.H. (1959) 'The bases of social power', in D. Cartwright (ed) *Studies of Social Power*, Ann Arbor, MI: Institute of Social Research, pp 150-67.

French, R. (1999) 'The importance of *capacities* in psychoanalysis and the language of human development', *International Journal of Psychoanalysis*, vol 80, pp 1215-26.

Friedman, R.B. (1973) 'On the concept of authority in political philosophy', in R.E. Flathman (ed) *Concepts in Social and Political Philosophy*, Basingstoke: Macmillan.

Gaffney, M. (2002) *Change from the Inside: A Study of Unpaid Community Workers*, London: Community Development Foundation/Standing Conference for Community Development.

Gamson, W. (1992) *Talking Politics*, Cambridge: Cambridge University Press.

Garmezy, N. (1983) 'Stressors in childhood', in N. Garmezy and M. Rutter (eds) *Stress, Coping and Development in Children*, Baltimore, MD: Johns Hopkins University Press.

Garmezy, N. and Rutter, M. (eds) (1983) *Stress, Coping and Development in Children*, Baltimore, MD: Johns Hopkins University Press.

Gaventa, J. (2006) 'Finding the spaces for change: a power analysis', *Institute of Development Studies Bulletin*, vol 37, no 6, pp 23–33.

George, V. and Wilding, P. (2002) *Globalization and Human Welfare*, Basingstoke: Palgrave.

Gilchrist, A. (2003) 'Community development in the UK: Possibilities and paradoxes', *Community Development Journal*, vol.38, no 1, pp 16-25.

Glen, A, Henderson, P., Humm, J., Meszaros, H. and Gaffney, M. (2004) *Survey of Community Development Workers in UK*, London: Community Development Foundation/.

Glendinning, C., Powell, M. and Rummery, K. (eds) (2002) *Partnerships, New Labour and the Governance of Welfare*, Bristol: The Policy Press.

Gramsci, A. (1971) *The Prison Notebooks* (ed and transl Quintin Hoare and Geoffrey Nowell Smith), London: Lawrence & Wishart.

Greig, A., Hulme, D. and Turner, M. (eds) (2007) *Challenging Global Inequality*, Basingstoke: Palgrave.

Halford, S. and Leonard, P. (1999) 'New identities? Professionalism, managerialism and the construction of self', in M. Exworthy and S. Halford (eds) *Professionals and the New Managerialism in the Public Sector*, Buckingham: Open University Press, pp 102-20.

Halford, S. and Leonard, P. (2005) 'Place, space and times: contextualizing workplace subjectivities', *Organization Studies*, vol 27, no 5, pp 657-76.

Hall, S. (1991) 'Old and new identities, old and new ethnicities', in A. King (ed) *Culture, Globalization and the World-System*, Basingstoke: Macmillan.

Hanly, C. (1984) 'Ego ideal and ideal ego', *International Journal of Psychoanalysis*, vol 65, pp 253-61.

Hayek, F. (1982) *Law, Legislation and Liberty*, London: Routledge.

Hebson, G., Grimshaw, D. and Marchington, M. (2003) 'PPPs and the changing public sector ethos: case-study evidence from the health and local authority sectors', *Work, Employment and Society*, vol 17, no 3, pp 481-501.

Heery, E. (1987) 'A common Labour movement? Left Labour councils and the trade unions', in P. Hoggett and R. Hambleton (eds) *Decentralisation and Democracy: Localising Public Services*, Occasional Paper 28, Bristol: School for Advanced Urban Studies, University of Bristol.

Hickey, S. and Mohan, G. (eds) (2004) *Participation: From Tyranny to Transformation?*, London: Zed Books.

Hoatson, L. (2003) 'The scope of Australian community practice', in W. Weeks, L. Hoatson and J. Dixon (eds) *Community Practices in Australia*, Frenchs Forest, Pearson Education.

Hochschild, A. (1983) *The Managed Heart: The Commercialisation of Human Feeling*, Berkeley, CA: University of California Press.

Hoggett, P. (1996) 'New modes of control in the public service', *Public Administration*, vol 74, no 1, pp 9-32.

Hoggett, P. (2000) *Emotional Life and the Politics of Welfare*, Basingstoke, Palgrave Macmillan, pp 22-44.

Hoggett, P. (2001) 'Democracy, social relations and ecowelfare', *Social Policy and Administration*, vol 35, no 5, pp 608-26.

Hoggett, P. (2005a) 'A service to the public: the containment of ethical and moral conflicts by public bureaucracies', in P. du Gay (ed) *The Values of Bureaucracy*, Oxford: Oxford University Press.

Hoggett, P. (2005b) 'Human emotion and ethical dilemmas', in A. Moran and S. Watson (eds) *Trust, Risk and Uncertainty*, Basingstoke: Palgrave.

Hoggett, P. (2006) 'Pity, compassion, solidarity', in S. Clarke, P. Hoggett and S. Thompson (eds) *Emotion, Politics and Society*, Basingstoke/New York: Palgrave Macmillan.

Hoggett, P., Mayo, M. and Miller, C. (2006) 'On good authority', *Socio-Analysis*, vol 8, pp 1-16.

Hoggett, P., Beedell, P., Jimenez, L., Mayo, M. and Miller, C. (2006) 'Identity, life history and commitment to welfare', *Journal of Social Policy*, vol 35, no 4, pp 689-704.

Home Office (2005) *Community Cohesion – An Action Guide: Guidance for Local Authorities*, London, Home Office.

Honig, B. (1993) *Political Theory and the Displacement of Politics*, Ithaca, NY: Cornell University Press.

Honig, B. (1996) 'Difference, dilemmas and the politics of home', in S. Benhabib (ed) *Democracy and Difference: Contesting the Boundaries of the Political*, Princeton, NJ: Princeton University Press.

Honneth, A. (1995) *The Struggle for Recognition: The Moral Grammar of Social Conflict*, Cambridge: Polity Press.

Hook, S. (1974) *Pragmatism and the Tragic Sense of Life*, New York: Basic Books.

Hopwood, A. and Miller, P. (1994) *Accounting as Social and Institutional Practice*, Oxford: Oxford University Press.

Hulme, D. and Edwards, M. (eds) (1997) *NGOs, States and Donors: Too Close for Comfort?*, Basingstoke: Palgrave.

Hutton, W. (1999) *The Stakeholding Society: Writings on Politics and Economics*, Cambridge: Polity Press.

Jasper, J. (1998) 'The emotions of protest: affective and reactive emotions in and around social movements', *Sociological Forum*, vol 13, no 3, pp 397-424.

Jasper, J. and Poulsen, J. (1995) 'Recruiting strangers and friends: moral shocks and social networks in animal rights and anti-nuclear protests', *Social Problems*, vol 42, no 4, pp 493-512.

Jeffs, T. (2004) 'Curriculum debate: a letter to Jon Ord', *Youth and Policy*, vol 84, pp 55-61.

Jeffs, T. and Smith, M. (2006) 'Where is *Youth Matters* taking us?', *Youth and Policy*, vol 91, pp 23-38.

Jessop, B. (2003) 'Governance and metagovernance: on reflexivity, requisite variety and requisite irony', in H. Bang (ed) *Governance as Social and Political Communication*, Manchester: Manchester University Press.

Kabeer, N. (2005) 'Introduction: the search for inclusive citizenship', in N. Kabeer (ed) *Inclusive Citizenship*, London: Zed Books, pp 1-27.

King, D. (2006) 'Activists and emotional reflexivity: towards Touraine's subject as social movement', *Sociological Review*, vol 40, no 5, pp 873-91.

Larsen, T., Taylor-Gooby, P. and Kananen, J. (2006) 'New Labour's policy style: a mix of policy approaches', *Journal of Social Policy*, vol 35, no 4, pp 629-49.

Lasch, C. (1977) *Haven in a Heartless World: The Family Besieged*, New York: Basic Books.

Lasch, C. (1979) *The Culture of Narcissism: American Life in an age of Diminishing Expectations*, New York: Norton.

Layard, R. (2005) *Happiness*, London: Allen Lane.

Lazarus, R. and Folkman, S. (1984) *Stress, Appraisal and Coping*, New York: Springer Publishing Company.

Le Grand, J. (2003) *Motivation, Agency and Public Policy*, Oxford: Oxford University Press.

Lipsky, M. (1980) *Street-level Bureaucracy: Dilemmas of the Individual in Public Service*, New York: Russell Sage Foundation.

Lister, R. (2004) *Poverty*, Cambridge: Polity Press.

London Edinburgh Weekend Return Group (1980) *In and Against the State*, London: Pluto Press.

Loney, M. (1983) *Community Against Government: The British Community Development Project, 1968–78, A Study of Government Incompetence*, London: Heinemann.

Loney, M. (1996) *The Politics of Greed: The New Right and the Welfare State*, London, Pluto Press.

Lovell, T. (2003) 'Resisting with authority: Historical specificity, agency and the performative self', *Theory Culture and Society*, vol 20, pp 1–17.

Lukes, S. (1974) *Power: A Radical View*, London: Macmillan.

Lukes, S. (1987) 'Perspectives on authority', in R. Pennock and J. Chapman, *Authority revisited: NOMOS XXIX*, New York: New York University Press (reprinted in J. Raz [ed] [1990] *Authority*, London: Basil Blackwell).

McAdam, D., McCarthy, J. and Zald, M. (1996) *Comparative Perspectives on Social Movements: Political Opportunities, Mobilizing Structures, and Cultural Framings*, Cambridge: Cambridge University Press.

McCarthy, J. and Zald, M. (1977) 'Resource mobilization and social movements: a partial theory', *American Journal of Sociology*, vol 6, pp 1212–41.

Maclachlan, K. (2008) 'Policy, politics and practice: adult education in Scotland', in *Reclaiming Social Purpose in Community Education*, Edinburgh: The Reclaiming Social Purpose Group., pp 17–21

McNair, S. (2006) 'How different is the older labour market?', *Social Policy and Society*, vol 5, no 4, pp 485–94.

Markova, E. and Black, R. (2007) *East European Immigration and Community Cohesion*, York: Joseph Rowntree Foundation.

Marris, P. and Rein, M. (1972) *The Dilemmas of Social Reform: Poverty and Community Action in the USA*, London: Routledge and Kegan Paul.

Marshall, T.H. (1950) *Citizenship and Social Class* (repr 1991), London: Pluto Press.

Marshall, T.H. (1963) *Sociology at the Crossroads*, London: Heinemann.

Marx, K. (1970) *Economic and Philosophic Manuscripts of 1844, edited, with an introduction by Struik, D.*, London: Lawrence & Wishart.

Mauss, M. (1954) *The Gift: Forms and Functions of Exchange in Archaic Societies* (trans I. Cunnison), London: Cohen & West.

Mayo, M. (ed) (1977) Women in the Community, London, Routledge and Kegan Paul.

Mayo, M. (2000) *Cultures, Communities, Identities*, Basingstoke: Palgrave.

Mayo, M. (2005) *Global Citizens*, London: Zed Books.

Mayo, M. and Craig, G. (1995) 'Community participation and empowerment: the human face of structural adjustment or tools for democratic transformation?', in G. Craig and M. Mayo (eds) *Community Empowerment: A Reader in Participation and Empowerment*, London: Zed Books, pp 1-11.

Mayo, M. and Robertson, J. (2003) 'The historical and policy context: setting the scene for current debates', in S. Banks, H. Butcher, P. Henderson and J. Robertson (eds) *Managing Community Practice*, Bristol, The Policy Press, pp 232-4.

Mayo, M., Hoggett, P. and Miller, C. (2007a) 'Navigating the contradictions of public service modernisation', *Policy & Politics*, vol 35, no 4, pp 667-81.

Mayo, M., Hoggett, P. and Miller, C. (2007b) 'Ethical dilemmas of front-line regeneration workers', in S. Balloch and M. Hill (eds) *Care, Citizenship and Communities: Research and Practice in a Changing Policy Context*, Bristol: The Policy Press, pp 75-88.

Mayo, M., Hoggett, P. and Miller, C. (2007c) 'Capacities of the capacity-builders: should training frameworks include ethical and emotional dimensions?', in J. Diamond, J. Liddle, A. Southern and A. Townsend (eds) *Managing the City*, London: Routledge, pp 133-45.

Mendus, S. (2000) *Feminism and Emotion*, Basingstoke: Macmillan.

Miliband, R. (1969) *The State in Capitalist Society*, London: Weidenfeld & Nicolson.

Miller, C. (1996) 'Public service trade unionism and radical politics', Aldershot, Dartmouth Publications.

Miller, C. (2004) *Producing Welfare: A Modern Agenda*, Basingstoke: Palgrave Macmillan.

Miller, C. and Ahmad, Y. (1997) 'Community development at the crossroads: A way forward', *Policy and Politics*, vol 25, no 3, pp 269-84.

Miller, C., Hoggett, P. and Mayo, M. (2006) 'The obsession with outputs: over regulation and the impact on the emotional identities of public service professionals', *International Journal of Work, Organization and Emotions*, vol 1, no 4, pp 366-78.

Miller, E. (1993) *From Dependency to Autonomy: Studies in Organisation and Change*, London: Free Association Books.

Miller, K., Bikholt, M., Scott, C. and Stage, C. (1995) 'Empathy and burnout in human service workers: an extension of a communication model', *Communication Research*, vol 22, no 2, pp 123-47.

Miller, S.M. and Rein, M. (1975) 'Community participation: past and future', in D. Jones and M. Mayo (eds) *Community Work Two*, London: Routledge and Kegan Paul, pp 3-24.

Mirowsky, J. and Ross, C. (1990) 'Control or defence? Depression and the sense of control over good and bad outcomes', *Journal of Health and Social Behaviour*, vol 31, pp 71-86.

Moon, S. (2005) 'The state of the youth service: recruitment and retention rates of youth workers in England', *Youth and Policy*, vol 88, pp 29-44.

Mouffe, C. (1993) *The Return of the Political*, London: Verso.

Murray, C. (1984) *Losing Ground*, New York: Basic Books.

Newman, J. (2001) *Modernizing Governance: New Labour, Policy and Society*, London: Sage Publications.

Newman, J. and Vidler, E. (2006) 'Discriminating customers, responsible patients, empowered users: consumerism and the modernization of health care', *Journal of Social Policy*, vol 35, no 2, pp193-209.

Nussbaum, M. (2000) *Women and Human Development: The Capabilities Approach*, Cambridge: Cambridge University Press.

Nussbaum, M. (2001) *Upheavals of Thought: The Intelligence of the Emotions*, Cambridge: Cambridge University Press.

Offe, C. (1984) *Contradictions of the Welfare State*, London: Hutchinson.

Oliver, B. (2006) 'Identity and change; youth working in transition', *Youth and Policy*, vol 93, pp 5-19.

Page, R. (2007) 'Without a song in their heart: New Labour, the welfare state and the retreat from Democratic Socialism', *Journal of Social Policy*, vol 36, no 1, pp 19-37.

Pateman, C. (1970) *Participation and Democratic Theory*, Cambridge: Cambridge University Press.

Pearlin, L., Lieberman, M., Menaghan, E. and Mullan, J. (1981) 'The stress process', *Journal of Health and Social Behaviour*, vol 22, pp 337-56.

Popple, K. (1995) *Analysing Community Work*, Buckingham: Open University Press.

Powell, M. (2000) 'New Labour and the third way in the British welfare state: a new and distinctive approach?' *Critical Social Policy*, February, vol 20, no 1, pp 39-59.

Pratchett, L. and Wingfield, M. (1996) 'Petty bureaucracy and woolly-minded liberalism? The changing ethos of local government officers', *Public Administration*, vol 74, pp 639-56.

Prime Minister's Strategy Unit (2007) *Policy Review: The Role of the State*, London: Prime Minister's Strategy Unit, Cabinet Office.

Puddephat, A. (1987) 'Local state and local community: the Hackney experience', in P. Hoggett and R. Hambleton (eds) *Decentralisation and Democracy: Localising Public Services*, Occasional Paper 28, Bristol: School for Advanced Urban Studies, University of Bristol.

Putnam, R. (2007) 'E pluribus unum: diversity and community in the twenty-first century', *Scandinavian Political Studies*, vol 30, no 2, pp 137-74.

Raz, J. (1979) *The Authority of Law: Essays on Laws and Morality*, Oxford: Clarendon Press.

Raz, J. (1990a) 'Introduction', in J. Raz (ed) *Authority*, London: Basil Blackwell.

Raz, J. (ed) (1990b) *Authority*, London: Basil Blackwell.

Raz, J. (2003) *The Practice of Value*, London, Clarendon.

Reddy, K. (2002) 'Citizen participation in local governance: Andhra Pradesh Region', Paper presented to Regional Workshop of PRIA, New Delhi, India, 9-10 July.

Rousseau, J.-J. ([1755]/1993) *The Social Contract and Discourses* (3rd edn), London: Dent.

Saks, M. and Allsop, J. (2007) 'Social policy, professional regulation and health support work', *Social Policy and Society*, vol 6, no 2, pp 165-77.

Seabrook, J. (1984) *The Idea of Neighbourhood*, London: Pluto.

Seebohm Report (1968) *Report of the Committee on Local Authority and Allied Personal Services*, London: HMSO.

Sen, A. (2002) 'Justice across borders', in P. de Grieff and C. Cronin (eds) *Global Justice and Transnational Politics: Essays on the Moral and Political Challenges of Globalization*, Cambridge, MA: The MIT Press.

Sennett, R. (1980) *Authority*, London: Faber and Faber.

Sennett, R. (1998) *The Corrosion of Character*, New York and London: W.W. Norton.

Sennett, R. (2003) *Respect: The Formation of Character in an Age of Inequality*, London: Penguin.

Sevenhuijsen, S. (1998) *Citizenship and the Ethics of Care*, London: Routledge.

Shaw, M. (2008a) 'Community development and the politics of community', *Community Development Journal*, vol 41, no 1, pp 24-36.

Shaw, M. (2008b) 'Policy, politics and practice: community development', in *Reclaiming Social Purpose in Community Education*, Edinburgh: The Reclaiming Social Purpose Group, pp 13-16.

Silverman, S. (1968) 'Review of Miller and Rice: systems of organization', *British Journal of Industrial Relations*, vol 6, pp 393-7.

Skeffington Report (1969) *People and Planning*, London: HMSO.

Skidmore, P., Bound, K. and Lownsbrough, H. (2006) *Community Participation: Who benefits?*, York: Joseph Rowntree Foundation.

Smith, A. (1995) *Nations and Nationalism in a Global Era*, Cambridge: Polity Press.

Snow, D. and Benford, R. (1988) 'Ideology, frame resonance, and participant mobilization', *International Social Movement Research*, vol 1, pp 197-217.

Snow, D., Rochford, B., Worden, S. and Benford, R. (1986) 'Frame alignment processes, micromobilization, and movement participation', *American Sociological Review*, vol 51, pp 464-81.

Social Exclusion Unit (1999) *Bridging the Gap: New Opportunities for 16-18 year olds Not in Education, Employment or, Training* Cm 4405, London: The Stationery Office.

Solomos, J. (2003) *Race and Racism in Britain* (3rd edn), Basingstoke: Palgrave Macmillan.

Sondhi, R. (1995) 'From black British to black European: A crisis of identity?' in S. Jacobs and K. Popple (eds) *Community Work in the 1990s*, Nottingham, Spokesman, pp 37-50.

Spencer, S., Ruhs, M., Anderson, B. and Rogaly, B. (2007) *Migrants' Lives Beyond the Workplace: The Experiences of Central and East Europeans in the UK*, York: Joseph Rowntree Foundation.

Steele, J. (1999) *Wasted Values: Harnessing the Commitment of Public Managers*, London: Public Management Foundation.

Symington, N. (1986) *The Analytic Experience*, London: Free Association Books.

Tandon, R. (2008) 'Participation, citizenship and democracy: Reflections on 25 years of experience', *Community Development Journal*, vol 43, no. 3, pp 284-96.

Tarrow, S. (1994) *Power in Movement: Social Movements, Collective Action and Politics*, Cambridge: Cambridge University Press.

Taylor, C. (1989) *Sources of the Self*, Cambridge: Cambridge University Press.

Taylor, C. and White, S. (2000) *Practising Reflexivity in Health and Welfare*, Buckingham: Open University Press.

Taylor, J. and Turner, J. (2001) 'A longitudinal study of the role and significance of mattering to others for depressive symptoms', *Journal of Health and Social Behaviour*, vol 42, pp 310-25.

Taylor, M. (2003) *Public Policy in the Community*, Basingstoke: Palgrave Macmillan.

Taylor, P. and Fransman, J. (2003) *Learning and Teaching Participation: Exploring the Role of Higher Learning Institutions as Agents of Development and Change*, Falmer: Institute of Development Studies.

Taylor-Gooby, P., Larsen, T. and Kananen, J. (2005) 'Market means and welfare ends: the UK welfare state experiment', *Journal of Social Policy*, vol 34, no 3, pp 573-92.

Tett, L. (2008) 'Rearticulating professional identity', in *Reclaiming Social Purpose in Community Education*, Edinburgh: The Reclaiming Social Purpose Group, pp 25-8.

Thompson, S. and Hoggett, P. (1996) 'Universalism, selectivism and particularism: towards a postmodern social policy', *Critical Social Policy*, vol 16, no 1, pp 21-43.

Titmuss, R. (1968) *Commitment to Welfare*, London: George Allen & Unwin.

Titmuss, R. (1971) *The Gift Relationship*, London: Pantheon Books.

Titmuss, R. (1974) *Social Policy: An Introduction*, London: George Allen & Unwin.

Turner, J. and Lloyd, D. (1999) 'The stress process and the social distribution of depression', *Journal of Health and Social Behaviour*, vol 40, pp 374-404.

UK Citizenship Survey (2007), produced by NetCen on behalf of Race Cohesion and Faith Research Unit, Department for Communities and Local Government.

Vickerstaff, S. (2006) '"I'd rather keep running to the end and then jump off the cliff": retirement decisions: who decides?', *Journal of Social Policy*, vol 35, no 3, pp 455-72.

Waddell, M. (1989) 'Living in two worlds: psychodynamic theory and social work practice', *Free Associations*, vol 15, pp 11-35.

Wakefield, H. and Purdue, D. (2007) 'Activist burnout: emotions in social movements', Paper presented to Cinefogo Workshop, Trento, Italy, 21-22 May.

Weber, M. (1968) *Economy and Society: An Outline of Interpretative Sociology*, Berkeley, CA: University of California Press.

Williams, B. (1973) *Problems of the Self*, Cambridge: Cambridge University Press.

Williams, B. (1981) *Moral Luck*, Cambridge: Cambridge University Press.

Williams, F. (1999) 'Good-enough principles for welfare', *Journal of Social Policy*, vol 28, no 4, pp 667-87.

Willis, P. (1978) *Learning to Labour: How Working Class Kids Get Working Class Jobs*, London: Gower.

Winnicott, D.W. (1976) *The Maturational Processes and the Facilitating Environment*, London: Hogarth Press.

Woodward, V. (2004) *Active Learning for Active Citizenship*, London: CRU, Home Office.

Yeatman, A. (2007) 'Varieties of individualism', in C. Howard (ed) *Contested Individualization*, Basingstoke: Palgrave Macmillan.

Young, I. (2000) *Inclusion and Democracy*, Oxford, Oxford University Press.

Young, M. and Willmott, P. (1957) *Family and Kinship in East London*, London: Penguin.

Index